MACMILLAN AND CO., Limited
LONDON · BOMBAY · CALCUTTA · MADRAS
MELBOURNE

THE MACMILLAN COMPANY
NEW YORK · BOSTON · CHICAGO
DALLAS · SAN FRANCISCO

THE MACMILLAN CO. OF CANADA, Ltd.
TORONTO

THE LIFE OF
THOMAS CRANMER

ARCHBISHOP OF CANTERBURY

BY

ANTHONY C. DEANE, M.A., F.R.S.L.

VICAR OF ALL SAINTS', ENNISMORE GARDENS
AND HON. CANON OF WORCESTER CATHEDRAL

MACMILLAN AND CO., LIMITED
ST. MARTIN'S STREET, LONDON
1927

COPYRIGHT

PRINTED IN GREAT BRITAIN
BY R. & R. CLARK, LIMITED, EDINBURGH

GENERAL PREFACE

THE intention of this series of studies of the lives of English bishops and priests is to suggest the significance of the man in the age in which he lived and in the movements within the Church with which he was concerned. It is the general editorial policy to select a biographer sympathetic with the character with whom he deals, since, in the view of the editor, sympathy is necessary to understanding. The choice of subjects is entirely arbitrary, following no chronological order and no settled plan, and the writers represent every school of thought in the English Church. Each volume is individual, and the writer alone is responsible for its judgements.

CONTENTS

CHAPTER VIII

CHAPTER IX

CHAPTER I

THIS book will attempt to describe, without political or ecclesiastical bias, a career than which none has been judged more variously, and a time unequalled for its lasting influence upon the character of the English Church.

The life of Thomas Cranmer comprised two periods. They were as curiously similar in length as they were tragically different in fortune. Fifty-three years lay before him when, a boy of fourteen, he quitted his mother and the rural home of his youth. Twenty-six were to be spent in the placid atmosphere of Cambridge. Twenty-seven were to be passed in the perilous forefront of public affairs. The former we may believe to have been years of increasing happiness. Their end found Cranmer admirably placed. His setting was of the kind exactly suited to his best qualities. His work was congenial, and not unimportant. If he were still unknown to the nation at large, he had won an honourable reputation in his University. He was accounted a man of personal charm, an erudite scholar, a theologian of liberal sympathies. He was no leader, for his views were ever apt to be indeterminate and to shift with the company in which he found himself. Yet, if hardly a commanding figure, Thomas Cranmer, Fellow of Jesus, had gained by his fortieth year a definite and respected place in the academic circles of Cambridge.

Beyond them he showed no desire to pass. He was notably free from ambition. He had never angled for ecclesiastical preferment. He viewed such practices with praiseworthy dislike. " Ye do know ", he wrote in later years to Cromwell, " what ambition and desire of promotion is in men of the church, and what indirect means they do use and have used to obtain their purpose ; which their unreasonable desires and appetites I do trust that ye will be more ready to oppress and extinguish than to favour or further the same ; and I remit to your wisdom and judgment, what an unreasonable thing it is for a man to labour for his own promotion spiritual."

At forty years of age, then, Cranmer's

future seemed to hold but limited possibilities. He might succeed to the Mastership of Jesus, and spend the remainder of his days in its comfortable lodgings. Or he might elect to take a College living, and, carrying off to some rural cure his remarkable library of patristic writings, devote his leisure to that liturgical work for which he had so unusual a genius.

Some such future might have been anticipated for him. That which actually befell was what no admirer could have anticipated, and no friend could have desired. A mere accident suddenly transformed his life. Within a few months he was the king's envoy on a diplomatic mission. Within a few years he was Archbishop of Canterbury. From quiet work where his abilities found full scope, he was forced to a conspicuous position for which he was strangely unfit. There was scarcely a quality needed for successful leadership of the Church under a Tudor monarch—strength of conviction, high courage, and tenacity of purpose—in which Cranmer was not lacking. Faults which might have seemed venial in a private citizen or College tutor jeopardised the whole welfare of the Church when they were exhibited by the Primate of England. Year by year his character degenerated under the strain which his responsibilities imposed. At the end his infirmity of will did not save him from a martyr's death, yet deprived him of the glory of martyrdom. Seldom can fortune have wrought a change more un-expected, ironic, and unkind than when it transferred Cranmer from Cambridge to Lambeth. It turned an amiable and success-ful scholar into an irresolute and ineffective archbishop. It set him in a place where his virtues were of little value, where his latent faults developed, where he was scarcely to know an hour's peace, until an unhappy life darkened at length to its dreadful close.

Thomas Cranmer, the sixth of seven children, was born at Aslockton in Notting-hamshire on July 2, 1489. His father was a country gentleman, possessing some landed property but little wealth. Having taught his son to sit a horse and to handle the cross-bow, he made over the rest of the educational task to the village parish-clerk and school-master. Conveniently economical as was this arrangement for the father, it proved most unhappy for the son, who " suffered much from the harsh and curst disposition of his master ". To this cause, perhaps,

psychologists may ascribe that cringing servility which, flogged into the boy at Aslockton,
still characterised the Archbishop when his
master—a bully not less truculent than the
parish-clerk—was the King of England. But
in 1501 Cranmer's father died. The widow
rescued her boy from the pedagogue whom
he described in after years as " marvellous
harsh and cruel ". In 1503 he was sent
to Jesus College, Cambridge. For another
reason also this year was fateful for Cranmer.
It witnessed the framing of the treaty for
the marriage of Henry, Prince of Wales, to
Katharine of Spain.

They who visit Cambridge to-day, with
its stately buildings, spacious courts, trim
lawns bordering an exiguous stream, and
prosperous streets displaying every luxury
for undergraduate purchasers, will not easily
realise the town to which Cranmer journeyed
in 1503. It was a dismal outpost on the
fringe of a morass. Here and there thin
crops struggled on reclaimed patches of land.
For the rest, the countryside on which it
looked forth was a vast area of marsh and
reeds. The Cam was swollen by innumerable tributaries from the undrained land.
Much of the town itself lay often under water,
the retreat of which left unsavoury mire in

every footway. At times the floods would sweep away one or other of the principal bridges. In winter dank vapours from the Fens shrouded the place for weeks together. Even in an age when little attention was paid to the laws of health, the insalubrious position of Cambridge was a frequent theme for unfavourable comment. It must be added, however, that some maintained this to be all in its favour as a place of education. Excessive bodily vigour, they urged gravely, led to waste of time in sport and recreation. The student was more likely to mind his books if he did not feel too well.

The buildings were very different from those of to-day. Jesus College, where Cranmer was to find his home for a quarter of a century, had been founded six years before his arrival. Its buildings replaced the dissolved convent of St. Rhadegund. A contemporary description of it as " near Cambridge " helps us to realise how restricted at this time was the area of the actual town. Queens' College also was praised as a quiet retreat, remote from the din of Cambridge itself. Of the Colleges standing to-day at the centre of the town, Trinity did not yet exist. A part of the spacious grounds destined to become its site was occupied by

a College named Michaelhouse. Between
Michaelhouse and the Hospital of St. John
—afterwards St. John's College—stood King's
Hall, a mansion serving as a hostel for wealthy
students. The domestic buildings of King's
College stood near the north-west corner of
the chapel, on ground now occupied by the
University Library. With the work of building the magnificent chapel little progress
had been made since the death of Henry VI.
Forty years after that date it was still un-
finished and roofless.

A number of religious houses were inter-
spersed among the colleges and hostels. The
property of the Carmelites adjoined Queens'
College. The important house of the
Dominicans stood where Emmanuel is now
situated. But by far the greatest of these
establishments, and probably the chief ornament of Cambridge at this period, was the
noble house of the Franciscans. It occupied
the present site of Sidney Sussex. Within
its buildings Parliament had met, in the
reign of Richard II. In them, as the most
regal of the town, the banquet was spread
for Henry VII. when he visited Cambridge
in 1506. At the overthrow of the religious
houses, the architectural beauty of this
Franciscan seat did not save it from destruc-

tion. Yet fragments of it may exist still, as
its stones and timbers were utilised for the
building of Trinity.

The religious houses had no formal link
with the University. They were owned and
controlled by the various monastic and
mendicant Orders. But a large proportion
of their inmates were students, who mingled
with the collegians at lectures and elsewhere.
Indeed, the influence of these foundations
upon the intellectual life of the University
was always strong, and often discordant.

A word should be added of the hostels.
Those who remember such of these places
as survived into the nineteenth century will
recollect that, in their latter days, they
accommodated undergraduates unable to meet
the expenses of College life. But in Cranmer's
time they fulfilled an opposite function. They
accommodated the wealthier students. The
Colleges provided free, or nearly free, board
and lodging. They had been founded for
men who could not afford a University
education without this help. Considerable
indignation was felt when the sons of the
well-to-do, who should have paid their way,
began to occupy rooms in College. A
preacher in 1550 assailed them from the
pulpit. Formerly they " did live of them-

selves in Ostles ", but now were " fayne to crepe into Colleges ", thus diverting to themselves benefits that had been designed for the poor. The point deserves note, because the fact that Cranmer became an inmate of Jesus College might be supposed to show that his mother was at least moderately affluent. On the contrary, it goes far to prove that she could not afford to pay for her son's maintenance.

Were we able to visit the Cambridge of 1503, perhaps nothing would strike us more forcibly, as we traversed its unpaved and unlighted streets, than the tender age of its undergraduates. We should meet them not singly, or wandering in friendly groups as they pleased, but in companies, shepherded always by a Master of Arts. Without this escort they were not permitted to pass beyond the College gates. Cambridge combined, in fact, the modern functions of a University and a Public School. Cranmer matriculated at fourteen, and this was a quite normal age. The undergraduates were subject to strict schoolboy discipline. They slept in bare dormitories, which served also as studies. All their frugal meals were taken in hall. They were soundly birched, not only for vices, but for deeds we should reckon virtuous. So late as Elizabeth's reign, a University decree enacted that any undergraduate caught bathing in a river, pond, or other water within the county of Cambridge should suffer a double flogging, first in his College hall, and again on the following day before the University. It seems possible that this decree may have been framed in the interests of anglers, for it is certain that angling was a recreation popular with students, secular and religious alike. " Town and gown " disputes over it were frequent. The Corporation legally possessed the river. Doubtless some of the burgesses looked to do well by the sale of pike, an expensive dainty, to the collegians. Fierce was their resentment at the spectacle of collegians gaily landing pike for themselves. Formal protests were made. Of course they were made in vain. Something more than the expostulations of a Town Council are needed to keep an undergraduate from his amusements or an angler from his sport.

We must turn to consider the intellectual life of Cambridge at the time when Cranmer began his residence. It was on the eve of a vast change. But of the coming change there were as yet few visible signs. At Oxford Colet's lectures on the Pauline Epistles,

with their dissidence from the accepted
methods of New Testament interpretation,
had thronged the seats and caused considerable stir. Erasmus also had visited Oxford,
though in the character of a pupil rather
than a teacher. But upon Cambridge the
official hold of scholasticism seemed as
strong as ever. No doubt the " new learning " was the theme of keen debate in court
and cloister, in chapter-house and combination room. Travellers had reported its
triumphant advance in Continental universities. But they had reported also the moral
degeneracy of southern Europe. Nowhere
had the new learning made its position good
with such swiftness as in Italy; and nowhere
had the standards of religion and morals
undergone so rapid and so alarming a decline.
To link these facts in the relation of cause and
effect was, no doubt, an error. Yet it was
a very natural error. It accounts for much
of the persistent hostility which the cause of
humanism had to encounter at Cambridge.
The opposition of the Friars, the bitterest
of all, might be set down to theological
animus. They feared, and with reason,
that the new learning would discredit the
intellectual foundations of their system. But
many of the University leaders viewed the

question from another standpoint. They were very little concerned with the relative merits of St. Augustine and St. Jerome. They were very greatly concerned with the characters of their pupils. If they were loth to alter the traditional course of study, that was much less because they wished to retain Duns Scotus and Aquinas than because they wished to keep out immorality and infidelity.

Before long, these views were to be modified by a better understanding of humanism and, even more, by personal contact with that great exponent of humanism, Erasmus. Meanwhile, Cranmer had to submit to the scholastic education which had come down from the Middle Ages. He must spend the best part of seven years over the futilities of the " trivium " and " quadrivium ". Its initial subject, " grammar ", doubtless he found congenial enough. " Grammar " implied more than the term signifies in modern usage. The grammarian had to be skilled not merely in the accidence and syntax of Latin, but in its translation and composition. In these accomplishments Cranmer became highly proficient. Many years later he showed that his dislike of scholasticism had not shaken his belief in the educational value of grammar. After an official visit to the Priory of Worcester, in 1534, one of his injunctions commanded the appointment of a teacher of grammar for the younger monks.

From grammar, however, the Cambridge arts student had to pass to logic, rhetoric, philosophy, arithmetic, music, geometry, perspective, and astronomy. Most of these subjects he had to study, not according to the latest knowledge of his own time, but as set forth by the schoolmen. The majority of their works were as intolerably pedantic in form as they were archaic and useless in matter. Cranmer " was nozzled ", to quote a contemporary of his, " in the grossest kind of sophistry ", and " in the dark riddles of Duns and other subtile questionists, to his age of twenty-two years ". Small, however, as was his relish for such studies, his industry in mastering them was great. It reaped its reward. In 1511 Jesus College elected Cranmer to a Fellowship.

Meanwhile he had witnessed important events in the life of Cambridge. Its leading spirit then, and for many years after—until, indeed, base conspiracy closed a noble life on the scaffold—was John Fisher. Though a competent scholar, his was no commanding intellect. But he possessed qualities which, more often than intellectual power, lead to rapid advancement in Church or State. With great personal charm he united strength of conviction and tenacity of purpose. He could appreciate in others mental abilities exceeding his own, and it was from him that Erasmus received encouragement and hospitality in Cambridge. Moreover, Fisher knew how to please people of importance, and, having gained their confidence, to make them subserve his plans. His promotion was extraordinarily swift. Three years after taking his M.A. degree he was Senior Proctor. In another three years he had been elected Master of Michaelhouse, and speedily revived the fortunes of that ancient college. His office of proctor brought him occasionally to the royal Court. Here he became the close friend and confessor of the king's mother, the saintly Margaret, Countess of Richmond. In 1501 he was Vice-Chancellor. He was the first holder of both the Divinity Professorship and the Preachership which Lady Margaret founded. In 1505 he became Bishop of Rochester, Chancellor of Cambridge University, and President of Queens' College.

In this year, under Fisher's influence, Lady Margaret transformed a grammar school into Christ's College. Next she planned to change the decaying and impoverished

Hospital of St. John into St. John's College. She died in 1509, but within two years her bequests had completed the work begun in her lifetime.   Thus by the time that Cranmer took his first degree he had seen two important Colleges added to the University.   During their construction Lady Margaret's "master of works" was a young man named Ralph Morice.   Afterwards he remained at Cambridge as a student, taking his M.A. degree in 1526.   Probably he was Cranmer's pupil. Certainly he became his close friend.   When fortune's unexpected caprice had changed the Fellow of Jesus into Archbishop, Morice entered his household as private secretary. That post he held for twenty years.   It was an   ideal   relationship.   Cranmer's   beliefs might shift in a fashion disconcerting to most of his friends, the clouds of adversity might darken about him, but nothing could weaken the admiration or shake the loyalty of Ralph Morice.   To his pious care we owe the best account of Cranmer's early years and a valuable collection of his correspondence.

Thus the benefactions of Lady Margaret, bringing Morice to Cambridge, were ultimately to enrich Cranmer's life.   They had also a more immediate result which must have made a deep impression on the rustic-bred undergraduate. In 1506, when Christ's College was newly completed, Henry VII. made a royal progress through Cambridge. He and his imposing retinue halted on the outskirts of the town. There he was welcomed by Fisher in a speech of daring flattery, eulogising the generosity of a king whose avarice had become a byword. There followed a banquet, a pause at Fisher's lodgings in Queens', and a circuit of the principal Colleges. The day must have lived in Cranmer's memory. As he watched the procession he saw, riding by the king's side, a sturdy boy of fifteen. Thus for the first time he looked on the future Henry VIII., who was to become the master of his destiny.

In the year 1511, Cranmer, as we have seen, was elected to a Fellowship at Jesus. Within twelve months he had forfeited and regained it. He lost it because, in the discreet words of Morice, " it chanced him to marry a wife ". Foxe, the martyrologist, editing the narrative with his usual bias, transforms " wife " into " a gentleman's daughter ", adding that Cranmer, in order " with the more diligence " to pursue his own work, " placed the said wife at an inn called the Dolphin ". It is unnecessary to uphold Cranmer's character by such prevarication.

In point of fact the girl, familiarly nicknamed
" Black Joan ", seems to have been a serving-
maid at the Dolphin. This inn, standing
where is now the junction of All Saints'
Passage and Bridge Street, was a convenient
house of call for thirsty students on their
way from Jesus to the centre of the town.
We must remember that Cranmer at this
time was not yet ordained, and little more
than a boy. We need not blame him over-
much for an entanglement with a barmaid.
It was not the first or last incident of the
kind in undergraduate life. His consequent
marriage clearly was one of necessity. Not
of choice would he have forfeited the Fellowship he had just gained, and, with it, his
means of subsistence.

Having lost his College rooms, he seems to
have lived for a time at the Dolphin. There
a blunder or a jest identified him as the
ostler, and the fable that he had actually been
an ostler was revived to discredit him long
after he had become Archbishop. He contrived to earn a small stipend by lecturing at
Buckingham (afterwards Magdalene) College.
But this must have been a period of privation
and unhappiness. Within a few months,
however, " Black Joan " died in childbed,
and her infant did not survive. Thereupon

C

Jesus College re-elected Cranmer to his Fellowship, and this matrimonial episode came to an end which, in the circumstances, cannot be thought unfortunate.

For another, and a very different, reason this year, 1511, was to have an important influence upon Cranmer's life. In October, under Fisher's auspices, Erasmus began to teach in Cambridge. He opened with a class for instruction in Greek. Soon Fisher had procured for him the Lady Margaret Divinity Professorship. Were we to judge merely from the account given in his own correspondence, we should suppose Erasmus to have been a failure at Cambridge. His letters abound with half-humorous grievances. Few students attend his classes. Fewer pay his fees. When his natural courtesy leads him to deprecate payment, these rascally undergraduates take him at his word. The Cambridge climate during the winter terms is abominable. Worst of all, he is expected to drink College beer instead of the Greek wine he loves.

After two years of these trials, Erasmus left Cambridge. Doubtless he was handicapped considerably by his ignorance of English. Inevitably, too, staunch champions of the old learning viewed his work with dis-

favour and put what obstacles they could in
his way. Yet the support of Fisher more
than balanced such enmity. Indeed, the
results of his visit were to prove both deep
and enduring. If the intimate friends he
made at the time were few, they were people
of importance, who influenced others in turn.
Moreover, it was in his quiet chamber at
Queens' College that Erasmus found leisure
to prepare his *Novum Instrumentum*, that
edition of the Greek New Testament which,
more than any other volume, aided the new
method of studying Holy Scripture. Cranmer
is not mentioned among his few intimate
friends at Cambridge. But a letter written
soon after the death of Archbishop Warham
shows that Erasmus counted Cranmer among
his disciples. This is confirmed by two
significant dates in the narrative of Ralph
Morice—a narrative clearly derived from
Cranmer himself. He records that in 1511
Cranmer definitely left the old learning for
the new, and that in 1516 he turned to the
systematic study of theology. In 1511 the
Greek class of Erasmus was begun ; in 1516
his *Novum Instrumentum* was published.

Thereafter for a considerable number of
years Cranmer devoted himself to patient
theological study. The books he collected,

a proportion of which are still extant, show by their number the range, and by their annotations the thoroughness, of his reading. In or about the year 1523 he was ordained, and took his D.D. degree. Then he was appointed to lecture by his College, and by the University to examine divinity students. In the latter post he distinguished himself, and not seldom disconcerted candidates, by his insistence upon knowledge of the actual Scriptures. Hitherto an acquaintance with ancient writings about the Bible had been deemed more necessary than acquaintance with the text of the Bible itself.

The period between 1523 and 1529, from his thirty-fourth to his fortieth year, was indubitably the happiest of Cranmer's life. As Fellow and Divinity Lecturer of Jesus he had attained a distinguished position. He was in easy circumstances, with an income derived from private pupils as well as from his University and College posts. Long afterwards, in a letter to Sir William Cecil, he contrasted his inadequate means as an Archbishop with his freedom from financial anxiety in Cambridge. Now " I pay double ", he complains, " for everything that I buy. I took not half so much care for my living when I was a scholar of Cambridge as I do at this present." Yet his Cambridge work was not unduly exacting. It afforded him his two chief desires—a margin of income for the purchase of books, and a margin of leisure in which to study them.

His academic reputation grew. No one credited him with genius, nor had he the gifts which, without genius, qualify a man for leadership in university life. He was a painstaking and erudite scholar. His judgement on liturgical questions and points of canon law carried especial weight. Perhaps the most striking compliment paid to his repute was an attempt to transfer him from the banks of the Cam to those of the Isis. In 1520 Wolsey had visited Cambridge. He came with a setting of characteristic magnificence. The town showed its sense of his greatness by a most unusual cleansing of the streets on the eve of his arrival. Cranmer may have been presented to him on this occasion, for Dr. Capon, Master of Jesus, had the privilege of Wolsey's friendship. Not long afterwards, when Wolsey desired to strengthen the staff of his new foundation in Oxford, he offered Cranmer a canonry at Cardinal's College. This Cranmer was wise enough to decline. Had he craved ecclesiastical preferment, he must have welcomed the chance of placing himself under Wolsey's patronage. He had no such desire. With his books, his study, and the Fellows' garden at Jesus he was well content.

At this time, too, the intellectual life of Cambridge was stimulating enough. Themes far above mere College gossip were debated eagerly in hall and combination room. The battle of the old and the new learning was not over before the battle between the old and the new theology began. In 1520 Luther had burnt the papal bull at Wittenberg. In 1521 the Lutheran treatises were burnt publicly in Cambridge. In the following year Henry VIII. put forth the document which gained for him, and all English monarchs after him, the title of Defender of the Faith. In 1523 Bishop Fisher, still Chancellor of Cambridge, followed the royal example by a book to refute the Lutheran heresy. His action helps to emphasise the difference between the scholastic and religious controversies. If the latter, in some degree, sprang out of the former, it brought not merely fresh combats but a new grouping of combatants. Men who, like Fisher, had been foremost in championing the new learning, were now among those fervently denouncing the new religion. A natural prudence may have helped to influence them. He who proclaimed himself a disciple of Erasmus had nothing worse than the ridicule of the scholastics to fear. But he who confessed his sympathy with Luther already, in the ominous phrase of the day, " smelled of the fire ".

None the less, Lutheranism increased. Its Cambridge adherents met at night in the White Horse Inn, which therefore was nicknamed " Germany ". They were, for the most part, a zealous rather than a distinguished band. The most prominent for a time was Dr. Barnes, an Augustinian prior, whose indiscretions hindered the cause he had at heart more than his undoubted eloquence helped it. Bilney, again, though conspicuous among the early adherents, was too eccentric a character to have much weight. Yet Bilney it was who gained for Lutheranism in Cambridge a man of very different calibre. A sensation almost comparable to that which, three centuries later, was to stir Oxford when Newman seceded to Rome must have been felt in Cambridge when Hugh Latimer, hitherto a fierce opponent of Lutheranism, was known to have accepted its tenets.

Of Cranmer's religious position at this stage we lack precise knowledge. We may be certain that he followed the Lutheran controversy with keen interest. But he neither ranged himself with the Reformers like Latimer nor assailed them like Fisher. Yet later utterances of his make it probable that as yet he was definitely on the orthodox side. If Latimer's defection shook him, he kept his misgivings to himself. That was prudent even in 1524. A rash sermon by Dr. Barnes at the end of 1525 and the circulation of Tyndale's New Testament, with its aggressive notes, in 1526 made the avowal of Lutheran sympathies far more dangerous. It is certain that Cranmer took no leading part on either side.

Close upon this controversy, however, came another in which he was destined to figure most prominently. In 1527 " the king's matter " began to be bruited abroad. The royal conscience professed itself uneasy over the royal marriage of eighteen years before. A papal dispensation had permitted Henry to marry his brother's widow. Was the dispensation valid ? If so, he and Katharine were united for life. If not, the form of marriage was null, and Henry remained free to wed whom he would. With that question, destined to agitate not merely England but the Continent for the

next five years, we must deal more fully in
the succeeding chapter. Here we may be
content to note its immediate effect upon
Cranmer at Cambridge. While Fisher upheld the dispensation, Cranmer attacked it.
He was a canonist, and canon law decreed
that the Pope could dispense from human
law but not from divine. And it was divine
law, Cranmer argued, which marriage with
a brother's widow had infringed. His conclusion was vitiated, as we shall have to
remark later, by his ignorance of one very
material fact. But the case for the king's
claim, as Cranmer saw and urged it in
Cambridge, was strong. And his judgement
as a canonist may have been reinforced by
a very human feeling derived from experience. Henry had married Katharine by no
choice of his own. Cranmer also in his
youth had known the inconveniences of a
forced marriage. The former husband of
"Black Joan" could sympathise with the
husband of Katharine. But Cranmer knew
nothing of the actual relations between
Prince Arthur and his nominal wife. He
knew nothing of Henry's "conscience" and
its true character. He knew not that Henry
proposed to replace Katharine by the sister
of a woman he had seduced. Such knowledge

was hidden from the guileless Cambridge don. Such knowledge, with more of the same calamitous kind, he was soon to acquire.

For in August 1529 his destiny was to be changed. It is curious to reflect that the change was brought about by a bacillus ; a change that influenced the fortunes of Church and State, and not those of Cranmer alone.

Term was over, but he had remained in residence at Cambridge, reading with two private pupils. A severe epidemic began to rage in the town. Cranmer therefore withdrew himself and his pupils to Waltham in Essex. To the same place came the king, in high dudgeon over the latest papal stratagem. In his train were two Cambridge heads of houses : Fox, Provost of King's, as almoner, and Gardiner, Master of Trinity Hall, as secretary. These two and Cranmer supped together. At first they discussed Cambridge affairs, of which Cranmer was able to give the latest news. Then their talk passed to " the king's matter ". Cranmer stated his views and made a suggestion. From that moment, little as he guessed it, his future was transformed. On the morrow he was to quit for ever the service of Cambridge, his kind mother through the past twenty-six years. He was to exchange its light and agreeable tasks for staggering responsibilities. He was to pass from its pleasant courts to a court of a very different kind—a court where a truculent Henry, an immature Edward, and an infamous Mary were in turn to control, to degrade, and to end his life.

CHAPTER II

No historical character can be understood rightly without regard to its setting of time and place. This is true even of men strong enough to control circumstance. It is doubly true of Cranmer, whom circumstance controlled. His surroundings must be studied, because they did not merely colour his life, but dominated it. By nature he was amiable, candid, and pious. During his years at Cambridge these natural qualities prevailed. Afterwards they were evident too seldom. No longer was he true to himself. He permitted external forces to direct his actions and even to shape his creed. Weakness made him the tool of unworthy masters, and a perverted loyalty kept him their willing tool. It was from the setting of his own life that he deduced a novel view of the Church's position ; a view as untenable in theory as it proved disastrous in practice. Thus a study of the outward conditions is essential to an understanding of Cranmer's public career. We may well begin by recalling the position of king, Church, and people at that fateful time when Henry VIII. and Cranmer met at Waltham.

Twenty years had passed since Henry's accession. No English monarch had begun his reign under happier auspices. For this he was indebted greatly to his father. When Bishop Fisher preached the funeral sermon of Henry VII., in the course of his eulogies he remarked that the late king had " treasures and riches incomparable ", and that " leagues and confederacies he had with all Christian princes ". Both tributes were well justified. The former, indeed, may have brought a grim smile to the faces of his hearers, who remembered by what ruthless exactions the " treasures and riches " had been wrung from unwilling subjects. Yet this had been part of a far-sighted policy. Henry VII. did not crave riches for his own pleasures. He was most frugal in his expenditure. Those who termed him a miser had ample evidence to support the charge. Yet he wished to accumulate wealth not for its own sake but in order to fortify the throne. As money passed from the coffers of the baronage into

the royal exchequer, power passed with it.
By the end of his reign he had achieved his
purpose. The dominance of the nobility
was over. Within twenty-four years of Bos-
worth Field the first Tudor had gained for
the crown such a strength and independence
as it had not known for centuries. It was
almost to an autocracy that Henry VIII.
succeeded. One institution alone remained
exempt from royal control. As yet the king
was not ruler of the Church.

Again, the " leagues and confederacies "
celebrated by Fisher were the fruit of Henry
VII.'s astute diplomacy. He was his own
foreign minister. No other could have been
more successful. His intuition and adroitness were perfect of their kind. In Ferdinand
of Spain, for example, he met no mean
opponent. Yet he mastered Ferdinand at
every turn of the game. His son came to
the throne of a country at peace with all
nations, and secure of powerful aid when war
should return.

This new ascendancy of England stirred
a new patriotism among the English people.
The national spirit was fostered also by the
rise to power of the new middle classes, and
the corresponding decline of the old inter-
national nobility. Henry VIII. would know

how to use this national spirit for his own purpose when the time came. At the beginning of his reign he himself must have seemed a pattern Englishman. He was strong in body, hearty of speech, a skilled tennis-player, a notable archer, a good swordsman. Gifts other than those of an athlete were his also ; he was a genuine music-lover and composer, he had read widely, he could write a treatise or deliver a speech in a style that owed none of its renown to court flattery. Power and wealth, as we have noted, he received by inheritance. His wife was not of his own choosing, yet Katharine was both affectionate and clever. As yet the king seemed well content with the match. From the first, too, he showed the Tudor knack of finding precisely the right men for the tasks he required of them. Fox was a clear-sighted adviser, Wolsey a superb foreign minister, More united learning with sagacity. The reign could scarcely have opened with brighter prospects.

That they darkened quickly was due to the effect of Henry VII.'s bequests on a man of Henry VIII.'s temperament. He had inherited wealth, and he squandered it. He had inherited power, and he misused it. Doubtless in the earlier years of his reign a prodigal extravagance increased rather than lessened his popularity. The nation was not sorry to see the money hoarded by a parsimonious father circulated freely by his son. Moreover, the new sense of national greatness looked with approval on the opulent and spectacular displays which Henry VIII. provided. His example was followed by his court. The magnificence of Wolsey became a byword. When the Earl of Northumberland crossed the Channel to fight in France, his personal equipment included a steward, a master of the household, a master of the horse, two chaplains, an usher, a herald, numerous servers and cupbearers, a pavilion furnished with hangings, silk cushions, a feather-bed, and silver plate ; he had a closed carriage drawn by seven horses, two chariots of eight horses apiece, four carts each drawn by seven horses, together with much else scarcely suggestive of a campaigner's hardships. As for the king himself, his profusion knew no bounds. For a while the nation stared and admired. Other feelings were roused, however, when at length even the reserves hoarded by Henry VII. began to dwindle, and Henry VIII. sought means of replenishing his purse at the nation's expense.

His autocracy also soon outwent the

bounds which his father had set. Henry VII. at his worst believed that the king existed for England. Henry VIII. at his best believed that England existed for the king. Having a giant's strength, he used it at first like a giant, and afterwards like an ogre. He told Marillac, the French Ambassador, that he had a miserable people to rule, but would quickly impoverish them so that they would be powerless to resist. By compelling Parliament to identify itself with his schemes he preserved for a while some semblance of constitutional action. There was a significant change in the official style by which Parliament addressed him. Early in the reign, as in the reigns of his predecessors, it was " Your Grace ". Before the end it had become " Your Sacred Majesty ". We need not suppose that Henry VIII. began with any definite theory of government other than that of getting his own way. But by degrees he shaped his ideas into a perfectly coherent scheme. We need not doubt that he honestly believed it to be for the nation's good. It was based upon the absolute despotism of the Crown. Parliament and the Church were to have no other functions than the king assigned them, and no other duties than to act as his executive. Any man or woman who

D

questioned this theory of absolutism was a traitor, to be beheaded. Any man or woman who differed from the religion authorised by the king was a heretic, to be burnt.

Such was the position Henry VIII. was destined to reach ; such the man whom the pliable Cranmer would have to serve. He had strong passions, tenacity of purpose, a complete lack of scruple, real intellectual force, and the knack of charming those whom he desired to conciliate. Given such a personality as Henry's on the one hand, given such a personality as Cranmer's on the other, and the result of their impact was certain. The weak must yield to the strong. Cranmer, indeed, was probably the one conscientious man in England who could accept Henry's theory of absolutism without demur. There would be frequent times when his own conscience and Henry's will pointed in opposite directions. Yet they caused Cranmer no real hesitation. A conscience which suggested disobedience to the king must be, he felt sure, a conscience misinformed.

Such, then, were the two principal characters in the earlier part of the story we have to narrate. In proportion as we discern them clearly, we shall follow the life of Cranmer under Henry VIII. with feelings in which censure, however just, will never be unmingled with compassion.

Before 1529 it had become evident that the king's views must bring about political changes. But there seemed little reason to suppose that they would affect the ecclesiastical system. In fact, the position of the English Church at this time seemed particularly stable. It was exempt from royal control, and there was as little sign of disturbance from within as from without. Lollardism, always suspect for its political colour, had become a spent force. The new Reformation movement of the Continent had gained little vogue in England. Lutheranism could claim no more than a few open adherents at the Universities, and fewer elsewhere. Secret sympathisers it may have won, but these had the sense, in view of the Defender of the Faith's utterance, to keep their opinions to themselves. There was no popular desire for doctrinal changes, and the English Church, though unquestionably weakened as a spiritual force, was virtually unchallenged as a national institution. Rude jests about the clergy in general, and about monks, nuns, and friars in particular, were common enough. They went the round of the country markets. They roused guffaws in every ale-house. Some found their way into print. The buffoonery doubtless was leavened by a perfectly right feeling that the Church had become too absorbed by worldly affairs and great possessions. Yet the writers go astray who interpret these attacks as proof of a widespread anti-clerical movement. Even so truculent an onslaught against the clergy as Simon Fish's *Supplication for the Beggars*, published in 1528, was designed as a caricature rather than as a serious portrait. Sir Thomas More wrote a reply to its " railing rhetoric ". But already, in his *Dialogue* of 1528, he had provided the best answer to popular attacks on the clergy, whether of this period or any other. A few lines from it may be quoted :

In reproach of them we be so studious that neither good nor bad passeth unreproved. If they be sad, we call them solemn ; if they be merry, we call them mad. If they keep few servants, we call them niggards. If they keep many, we call them pompous. If a lewd priest do a lewd deed, then we say, lo ! see what sample the clergy giveth us, as though that priest were the clergy. But then forget we to look what good men be therein, and what good counsel they give us, and what good ensample they show us. But we fare as do the ravens and the carrion crows, that never meddle with any quick flesh, but where they may find a dead dog in a ditch, thereto they flee and thereon they feed apace. Let

a good man preach, a short tale shall serve us
thereof, and we shall neither much regard his
exhortation nor his good examples. But let a lewd
friar be taken with a wench, we will jest and rail
upon the whole order all the year after.

It must be owned, however, that the
monastic system had become a very serious
problem for the English Church. Wolsey
had recognised its gravity, had taken some
steps to deal with it, and doubtless intended
to take others so soon as he should be free to
turn from foreign politics to home affairs.
That day never came. Other and more
sinister figures would knock at the monastic
gates. The religious houses were to be not
mended but ended.

To that tragedy we shall have to return.
At the time now under review, the Church
seemed secure. Despite some criticism of
the secular clergy, despite some ill-natured
envy and some good-natured banter of the
religious, there was no strong anti-clerical
feeling. There was, if as yet latent rather
than clearly expressed, a strong feeling against
the Pope. It was, however, wholly political.
It was directed not against a spiritual leader
but against an Italian prince. With the
religious doctrines which the Pope held,
Englishmen, as a body, had no quarrel. With

the constant interference which the Pope claimed to exercise in English affairs, and with the vast sums drawn by papal officials from English pockets, popular discontent was emphatic. As the national spirit developed, this resentment became more acute.

From the seventh century onwards the English Church had resisted, at various junctures and with varying degrees of success, the attempted dominance of Rome. But in early days the claim of papal authority was based on spiritual grounds. Afterwards the spiritual influence of Rome declined in proportion as the Pope concerned himself increasingly with political intrigues. For the head of a world-wide Church was substituted the ruler of a petty Italian state. Political ambitions brought the papacy to disaster. Through seventy years the Pope was an exile in France. Between 1378 and 1414, two, and even three, men were each claiming at the same time to be the only genuine Pope. Such a state of affairs did not foster respect for the papacy. A formal ending of the schism was reached in 1414, but by the end of another century the Popes had done little to restore the prestige of their office. The best were astute politicians. The worst were notorious profligates. The

infamous record of Alexander VI., who had
procured election in 1492, was not forgotten
in Henry VIII.'s reign.   Julius II., by whom
the dispensation for Henry's marriage with
Katharine had been granted, set himself to
increase his territory at the expense of
other Italian princes, and led his troops to
battle.   It is scarcely surprising that England,
and indeed all Christendom, failed to reverence such characters as the successors of
St. Peter.   To show respect for spiritual
authority had been one thing.   To be mulcted
heavily for the benefit of an ambitious Italian
prince and his crew of corrupt officials was
quite another.

The facts here summarised are important
for our understanding of later events.   Despite
popular feeling, before 1527 there seemed
little sign of a breach with Rome.   Englishmen, as their habit is, grumbled but paid.
The king's relations with the Pope were
more than usually cordial.   Clement VII.
was his friend, to whom he had offered the
see of Worcester.   The royal attack on
Lutheranism had gratified Clement.   But
when a sudden change came, and Henry,
for his own nefarious purpose, desired to
break with Rome, he had no need to create
an anti-papal feeling among his subjects.

Such a feeling existed already. It was no less strong because it had seldom become articulate. The king's end was odious to all Englishmen. But the means he employed to gain it, the overthrow of the papal authority, seemed merely to effect a change which the great majority of Englishmen desired. Not until it had been made did the Church realise that occasional interference had been replaced by a continuous tyranny, and that the king's belief in the papal system was unshaken—provided only that in future the Pope was to be not Clement VII. but Henry VIII.

We cannot wonder that the anti-papal sentiment in the first quarter of the sixteenth century had been fostered by the inordinate greed of the papal lawyers. Their annual receipts from England had become exceedingly large. The preamble to the Dispensations Act of 1534 declares that " your subjects of this your realm, and of other countries and dominions being under your obeisance, by many years past have been, and yet be, greatly decayed and impoverished by such intolerable exactions of great sums of money as have been claimed and taken out of this your realm, and other your said countries and dominions, by the Bishop of Rome called

the Pope, and the see of Rome ", and proceeds to recite some twenty forms of such
payments, together with " other infinite sorts
. . . the specialities whereof be over long,
large in number, and tedious here particularly to be inserted ".

No doubt allowance should be made for
the rhetorical character of such statements.
The payment of " Peter's pence " is named as
one of the papal exactions, and accordingly
the poor of Henry VIII.'s reign have been
represented as groaning under this burden.
In point of fact, some centuries earlier this
individual tax had been commuted for an
annual payment of £200 by the State. Yet,
when all deductions have been made for
exaggeration, it remains true that the financial
demands of the Roman Church were ex-
orbitant and the anger they stirred considerable. The clergy were the chief sufferers.
Yet almost every Englishman of the upper
or middle classes was compelled at some time
in his life to apply to the papal court. He
found the business both tedious and expensive. Communication with Rome was slow.
Legal process at Rome was slower. At
every turn was an official, and every official
claimed a fee. In contested cases the chances
of a litigant depended upon the depth of his

purse. When personages of high rank were involved, bribes, secret influence, and political expediency far outweighed abstract justice in deciding the issue.

From no other source did the papal lawyers derive so rich a revenue as from matrimonial dispensations. In theory a dispensation was a relaxation of ecclesiastical law granted by the Pope to remove hardship from some particular case. In practice, it had become the normal prelude to marriage among people of rank. In theory, the marriage laws were extremely complex and wholly inflexible. In practice, there was hardly a marriage that could not be made, and none that could not be annulled, by means of a dispensation. To appreciate the working of this system, we have to remember that the prohibited degrees went far beyond their modern limits. Relationship or affinity to the fourth degree constituted a bar. Sponsorship was treated as relationship. The English population was small. The aristocracy which intermarried was but a small part of the population. Some kind of connection could be traced between almost all the great families. With the best will in the world, people were often puzzled to know whether the marriage they contem-

plated might not infringe some technical
prohibition. If it did, at whatever date the
flaw was discovered, their marriage would be
declared void and their children illegitimate.
Obviously it was a wise precaution to obtain
before marriage a dispensation, by which all
impediments, known or unknown, were set
aside.

This, however, was not the only market
which the papal lawyers found for their
wares. Oddly enough, dispensations had
to be sought on the one hand by persons
who wished their union to be stable, and on
the other by those who desired a marriage
terminable at will. In theory the sacrament
of marriage was indissoluble. Divorce was
unknown to the law, and historians who use
that word in connection with Henry VIII.
permit themselves an anachronism. People
validly married by the Church were tied for
life. There was a method, however, by
which those of lax views could ensure in
advance a way of escape. They too would
obtain a dispensation for their union. If
the time came when they wished to end it,
they had merely to prove that the dispensation had been granted in ignorance of some
material fact. The officials at Rome who
had procured the granting of the dispensa-

tion were ready enough, in consideration of another fee, to discover a flaw in it. Thereupon, as the dispensation was pronounced invalid, the marriage dependent upon it was automatically annulled, and both parties to it were regarded by the law as still unwed. Whether, then, he were religiously minded and eager to shun all risk of sin, or profligate and loth to contract any tie he could not break at will, almost every Englishman of good family obtained a dispensation for his marriage, and the papal coffers were well filled.

The virtual control of royal marriages by the dispensation system was perhaps the chief asset of the papacy. It brought not merely fees more than ordinarily lucrative, but great political power. A prince's marriage was an event of high importance, affecting always the succession to the throne in his own country, and often the relations between his own country and others. The Pope was able to facilitate or thwart such a marriage as best suited his own policy. In course of time this became intolerable to the English spirit. The average Englishman had found by his own experience that the methods of the papal courts were both cumbrous and costly. He had been ready enough to pay tribute to spiritual authority, but he was far less ready to pay fees to an Italian politician. And he did not see why the affairs of his own nation, and the alliances of his own ruler, should be subject to interference from outside. The old ecclesiastical view of the marriage law, for all its inconveniences, could claim his obedience as a son of the Church. But if in future the marriage laws were to be regulated by political expediency instead of religious principle, at least the interests of the King of England had a better claim to be studied than the interests of the Bishop of Rome.

Thus the changed character of the papacy, the practical working of the dispensation system, and the development of a national spirit in England have all to be taken into account when we review " the king's matter " —that crisis in the career of Henry VIII. which was to involve so deeply the fortunes of Thomas Cranmer. To the story of that sordid but remarkable episode we can now turn.

For reasons of political advantage and a splendid dowry, in 1501 Henry VII. had contrived a match between his son Arthur and Katharine, daughter of Ferdinand of Aragon. Owing to the bridegroom's ill-health, the marriage was not consummated, and Arthur, a boy of fifteen, died within four months of his wedding. Thereupon Ferdinand, who as yet had paid over only one-third of the dowry, demurred to paying the rest. This did not suit the English king. He wanted the whole of the dowry ; he wanted also the political strength promised by an alliance with Spain. Therefore he proposed that his son Henry, then eleven years of age, should replace Arthur and be betrothed to Katharine. A dispensation was needed, and a dispensation to allow marriage with a sister-in-law was felt to be rather beyond the common. Ultimately it was granted, however, by Pope Julius II., and in the widest terms, expressly sanctioning the union whether or no the previous marriage of Katharine to Arthur had been consummated. In the year of his accession to the throne Henry of England married Katharine of Spain.

For a time all went well. Katharine was virtuous, attractive, and clever. When Henry was out of the country on his French wars, she filled his place as regent with notable spirit and success. The king's temperament, however, did not permit him to be faithful for long. Within ten years of his marriage he had an illegitimate child by

Elizabeth Blount. Soon afterwards he was attracted by the daughters of Sir Thomas Boleyn. Mary Boleyn he seduced. Anne Boleyn he desired to treat in the same fashion. But Anne united her sister's lax morality with an ambitious and calculating spirit of her own. She knew that Henry had begun to tire of Katharine. Therefore she refused to gratify the king's passion except on terms. Her attitude had the effect upon which she had counted. It increased Henry's admiration of her and strengthened his resolve. No obstacle could stand between him and anything he desired. He must add Anne Boleyn to his possessions. If she stipulated for marriage as the price of her surrender, marriage she should have. That he was already equipped with one wife was regrettable, yet it need not hinder him from supplementing her with another. He would obtain from the Pope a licence for bigamy. A privilege conceded to the patriarchs could scarcely be denied to Henry Tudor.

Amazing as it seems, this was the king's quite serious resolve. He had already instructed his agent at Rome to apply for the licence when the horrified Wolsey intervened. He could gain the abandonment of this project only by promising his support for an alternative which seemed to the king, on reflection, even more desirable. After all, it might be better to get rid of Katharine. Her beauty was waning, and she had failed to bear the son desired in order to safeguard the succession. Therefore the marriage with her must be annulled. The dispensation sanctioning it must be found invalid. That should be easy, since the hesitation over granting it had been considerable, and many learned canonists—of whom Cranmer was one—held that Julius II. had exceeded his dispensing powers by permitting union with a sister-in-law. Accordingly, Henry caused it to be known that his conscience was sorely disquieted by the possible illegality of his marriage with Katharine, and that he ardently desired Pope Clement VII. to reconsider the action of Pope Julius II.

Certain historians have argued that Henry's qualms may have been genuine. However improbable, it is, of course, not impossible that a conscience which lay dormant through seventeen years of marriage suddenly asserted itself in the eighteenth. But Henry's apologists overlook a fact which unfortunately leaves no doubt of his real character. We have seen that he had guilty relations with

Mary Boleyn. Now he proposed to wed Mary's sister. But she in the eyes of ecclesiastical law occupied the same position as Katharine had done. There had been suppositious marital relations between Katharine and Henry's brother. There had been actual marital relations between Henry and Anne's sister. The conscience which was so belatedly perturbed by union with one sister-in-law now proposed to find peace through union with another. All Henry's contemporaries who were conversant with the facts of the case regarded his plea of a troubled conscience as a piece of blatant hypocrisy. And it is impossible to doubt that they were right.

Sordid as " the king's matter " was, this detailed account of its origin has seemed necessary in order that we may apprehend the part taken by Cranmer in its final stages. But its development prior to his appearance may be summarised briefly.

Henry made his application to the Pope. In normal circumstances it would have been granted readily enough. The ecclesiastical difficulty of reversing a predecessor's decision would have been more than balanced by the political advantage of the King of England's friendship. The dispensation of Julius would have been revoked, the marriage with Katharine annulled, the marriage with Anne permitted. But, unhappily for the king, the circumstances at this moment were far from normal. Pope Clement VII.'s schemes had brought him into collision with the emperor, and he was virtually a prisoner in Rome. The emperor, Charles V., was Katharine's nephew. Not if he could help it should his aunt be thrown aside by the royal libertine of England. So close was the guard kept upon the Pope that there was considerable delay before Henry's application could reach him. When it arrived, it placed Clement in a most uncomfortable dilemma. He would much have preferred to obey the wishes of Henry, who was his friend, rather than those of Charles, who was his enemy. But Henry was at a distance in England. Charles with a powerful army was at his door. He desired to please the king. He was afraid to displease the emperor. Therefore he took the only course which, in these circumstances, seemed possible. He temporised. If movements by the French should succeed in weakening the pressure of Charles's army, it might become practicable to comply with Henry's request. As yet, however, it was not. Therefore he played, with considerable adroitness, a waiting game. At moments he seemed to step forward and to reach the verge of a decision in Henry's favour. Promptly Charles growled, and the step timidly taken was hastily withdrawn.

At last it seemed as though an end were in sight. Cardinal Campeggio, much against his will, was despatched by Clement to England, where he and Wolsey, as joint legates, were empowered to hear the case. The court was duly convened. Katharine appeared, but only to enter a dignified refusal to plead. Already she had affirmed her union with Arthur to have been one of form alone. She denied the jurisdiction of Wolsey and Campeggio, claiming that she, like Henry, must have an opportunity of placing her case before the Pope himself, to whom she had appealed. Having said this, she withdrew. The eager cheers greeting her in the streets and the groans that assailed Campeggio showed plainly enough the verdict of the English people. In private both Campeggio and Wolsey implored the king to abandon his proceedings. They implored in vain. Yet the tender conscience which, as he alleged, constrained him to persevere with his suit, did not deter him from insulting Katharine or from cohabiting openly with Anne Boleyn. Month after month the matter dragged on. Campeggio had arrived

in October 1528. By July 1529, despite
Henry's efforts to intercept the message, the
Pope had received Katharine's formal appeal
and the original brief issued by Julius II. He
could not ignore them. Campeggio had to
announce that the hearing in England was
suspended, to be resumed, at some quite in-
definite future, in Rome.

Thereupon Henry's patience, never the
strongest feature of his character, gave way.
He was furious with the Pope, who had
tricked him. He was even more furious with
Wolsey, whose advice had enabled him to be
tricked. No such humiliation, he felt, could
have befallen him had he pursued his original
idea, and, instead of working elaborately for
separation from one wife, had simply obtained
a licence to have two. Almost beside himself with anger and disappointment, he left
London, and, accompanied by Fox and
Gardiner, withdrew to Waltham Abbey.
There, as we have seen, his companions
chanced to meet Thomas Cranmer, and discussed with him the situation. He did not
hesitate to say that it had been mishandled,
"especially for the satisfaction of the troubled
conscience of the king's highness. For in
observing the common process and frustratory
delays of these your courts, the matter will

linger long enough ; and peradventure in the end come to small effect." That, to judge from the events of the previous nine months, seemed highly probable. Then Cranmer offered Fox and Gardiner a suggestion of his own. A proposal had been made already of collecting opinions on " the king's matter " from the universities of Europe. These, if favourable, could be used to strengthen his case in the papal court. And such favourable opinions, as Cranmer remarked with some cynicism, could be obtained " with little industry and charges ". But he suggested further that, when obtained, these opinions should be put to a use far more conclusive than as yet had been intended. Why trouble to lay them before the Pope ? Let them be taken as decisive. Let a judgement based upon their collective wisdom be given by the English Archbishop, without further reference to the Bishop of Rome. Thus the matter would be settled, a useful precedent created, and, with little delay or expense, " the troubled conscience of the king's highness " would be eased of its pangs.

Fox and Gardiner hurried to place this idea before the king. They had reason to welcome any suggestion which might distract his mind and soothe his temper. Yet, being uncertain how he might receive it, they were careful to explain that the project was not their own but Cranmer's. But Henry welcomed it with enthusiasm. He was no less enthusiastic about its author. " This man hath the sow by the right ear ",[1] he exclaimed. Cranmer was summoned to his presence. A man at once ingenuous enough to believe in the royal conscience and ingenious enough to further the royal aims was indeed one to be welcomed. From that day he was in the king's service. It was an irony of fortune which made this advancement partially due to Gardiner, the very man who in later years was to prove his most implacable enemy.

With the unerring knack of character-reading which distinguished the Tudors, Henry did not merely see that Cranmer was an instrument whom he could employ. He saw also that here was a man extremely susceptible to influence and easily swayed by his surroundings. Therefore surroundings of the right kind must be provided for him. As yet he must not be placed at court, where plain truths were whispered about the king's conscience and the king's morals. He must not mix with the general public, which

---

[1] " The right sow by the ear " seems to be a later and less authentic version.

was whole-heartedly in favour of Katharine. With consummate adroitness, Henry billeted Cranmer upon Anne Boleyn's father. An inmate in that household would be safe from contaminating influence. He would hear but one side of the case. Anne herself, when released for a time by her royal paramour, could practise upon Cranmer those arts of fascination which had charmed Henry. His leisure could be occupied in composing a treatise on the limits of papal dispensations. It might help to convince the University of Cambridge. Certainly it would keep its writer out of harm's way.

If Henry quitted Waltham no less irate with the Pope than he came, and no less furious with Wolsey, at least he could feel that his sojourn there had not been profitless. A happy chance had brought him a new policy and a new agent. This Cambridge don, equally simple and subservient, as credulous as he was learned, could be accounted henceforth a tool added to the king's store. He should be used to the full when opportunity served.

CHAPTER III

CRANMER was not the only new servant gained
by Henry VIII. in 1529. In the same year
he acquired the aid of a very different man;
ambitious as Cranmer was modest, resolute
as Cranmer was vacillating, and unscrupulous
as Cranmer, with all his faults, was devout.
Thomas Cromwell was reputed to be the son
of a Putney blacksmith. His youth had
been adventurous and disreputable. After
many vicissitudes of fortune at home and
abroad, in the course of which he had been
soldier, wool-merchant, money-lender, and
lawyer, he entered the service of Wolsey, and
discharged tasks which his master wished to
be done but was loth himself to do. Within
three months of Henry's meeting with Cranmer, Wolsey was deprived of the chancellorship. Cromwell defended him in the House
of Commons, and succeeded in averting for a
time the final blow, to fall a year later when

the Cardinal was arrested on a charge of
treason. Before the end of 1529, however,
it was clear that Wolsey's day was over.
Thereupon Cromwell contrived to attach
himself to the king. He whispered a suggestion which developed drastically the idea
already put forward by Cranmer. If the
Pope still proved obdurate, urged Cromwell,
let the king renounce all allegiance to him.
Let the Head of the English State declare
himself also the Head of the English Church.
Thus his power would be consolidated. An
end would be put to Italian interference with
English domestic affairs. A large revenue
hitherto sent overseas would find a far more
appropriate place in the king's purse. Henry
could contract any marriage he desired without hindrance.

Such a policy had obvious attractions for
the king. Yet its difficulties also were
obvious to him, as probably they were not
to Cromwell, a plebeian unversed in high
politics. A change of so revolutionary a
kind could only be attempted after careful
preparation. Parliament must be cajoled or
coerced into obeying orders. The Church
must be terrorised. Convocation must be
silenced. Otherwise the passage of the necessary legislation would be doubtful. It was

true that by this time the English people, as a whole, had no love of the papal system. But it was also true that they regarded their sovereign's matrimonial intrigue with positive disgust, and if he proclaimed his wish to overthrow the Pope's authority, they would have no doubt of his real motive. Moreover, Henry himself, except for the financial gain suggested by Cromwell, was reluctant to break finally with the Pope. Anti-papal action by him in England might seem to argue sympathy with the anti-papal movement on the Continent, a movement which, with its religious views, he detested. He might be driven later into carrying out Cromwell's suggestion. Whether that became necessary must depend on the Pope himself. If he would give his decision, and give it on the right side, there need be no conflict. One thing, however, was certain. With the help of the Pope, or in spite of the Pope, Henry VIII. must wed Anne Boleyn.

Such being his view of the future and its various chances, the king shaped his immediate plans with consummate skill. He would not yet despair of gaining the papal decision he required. Yet another mission should be despatched to restate his case. Meanwhile, progress should be made with

Cranmer's scheme of obtaining opinions from the Universities. Parliament should be summoned, kept in session, and taught that its function was to ratify the king's wishes. Its initial task should be an attack upon some minor privileges and revenues of the Church. Legislation of this type would fulfil a double purpose. It would prepare the way for more drastic measures if the Pope yet hardened his heart and recourse to Cromwell's suggestion became necessary. It would be a step in the direction of asserting the king's ecclesiastical supremacy. Also it might serve to make that action needless. It would show that the king was very much in earnest, and be a threat with which the envoys to Rome could back their arguments. It might convince the Pope that, whatever the difficulty of granting Henry's demands, worse things would happen if he still refused.

Before the close of 1529 the envoys had begun their journey. The choice of their leader was such as none but Henry could have made. Actually he selected Thomas Boleyn, now promoted to the earldom of Wiltshire. Among his company went Cranmer, who, as we have seen, had been his guest for some months. The presence of Anne's father would show the Pope how fixed was the king's purpose. The presence of Cranmer would enable him to hear the king's case set forward by a skilled canonist. Possibly, too, the choice of envoys may have been influenced by a wish that Cranmer should be out of England for the next few months. The suggestion he had made at Waltham was now to be carried into effect. The opinions of the Universities were to be obtained. But it might be as well that Cranmer, whose links with Cambridge were so recent and intimate, should not witness the methods used to obtain them.

The question propounded to the University divines was " whether a man may lawfully marry his brother's wife, after that brother's death without issue ". Henry took care that they should be left in no doubt either of the answer they had to give or of the consequences to themselves should they prove recalcitrant. The task of seeing the business through at Cambridge was left to Fox and Gardiner. To Oxford he wrote, in a preliminary letter : " And in case you do not uprightly, according to divine learning, humble yourselves herein, ye may be assured that we, not without great cause, shall so quickly and so sharply look to your unnatural misdemeanour herein, that it shall not be to your quietness and ease hereafter." Of the Cambridge proceedings we have an account, both vivid and cynical, in a long despatch from Fox and Gardiner to the king. The vice-chancellor took their side. But the opposition was active. " As we assembled, they assembled ; as we made friends, they made friends ; to let that nothing should pass as in the university's name." A "grace" for the appointment of a commission of divines to report, in the University's name, on "the king's matter" was put forward. It was defeated. It was put forward again, and the votes were equal. " At the last, by labour of friends to cause some to depart the house which were against it, it was obtained." The letter ends with a list of the commissioners ; a mark is set against the names of such as may be expected to support the king. " Your Highness may perceive by the notes that we be already sure of as many as be requisite, wanting only three ; and we have good hope of four ; of which four if we get two and obtain another to be absent, it is sufficient for our purpose."

Another month's intriguing, however, proved necessary to secure this result. Even then, the decision issued was really fatal to the king's claim. It pronounced marriage with a deceased brother's wife to be illegal if the former marriage had been consummated —which, in fact, the union of Arthur and Katharine had not been. It was a necessary part of Henry's case, however, that Katharine had perjured herself on this point. Thus he professed great delight at the Cambridge judgement. The vice-chancellor, who conveyed it to Windsor, was rewarded with a gift of money. But the welcome given by the king was not echoed by the courtiers. They knew nothing of canon law, papal precedents, or interpretations of Leviticus. They did know Henry and Katharine, the one for a gross hypocrite, the other for a cruelly wronged wife. If their feelings had to be hidden from the king, it would be some consolation to show them quite plainly to this visitor from Cambridge, and they were feelings endorsed by the nation at large. Despite the king's gift, the vice-chancellor had little reason to enjoy his stay at Windsor. " I was glad that I was out of the Court," he wrote to a colleague soon afterwards, " where many men, as I did both hear and perceive, did wonder on me. All the world almost crieth out at Cambridge for this act."

Oxford proved more obstinate than Cambridge. Much time had passed and many

royal threats had been applied before a decision in the king's favour could be wrung
from it, and the majority was but one of five
votes. Thus his appeal to the English Universities did the king little good. He could
claim that the decisions given were technically
in his favour. Yet the reservations qualifying
them were so considerable, and the pressure
used to obtain them so notorious, that in this
country their forensic value was as slight as
their moral weight. Abroad they could be
turned to some use. Their example helped
to secure opinions favourable to the king
from seven of the continental universities.
Others among them hesitated. Yet others
had more to fear from the emperor than from
the king, and decided accordingly.

Meanwhile, this preliminary business had
brought Henry a warning which he was quick
to note. The Church in his own land had
shown signs not merely of alarm and dismay,
which mattered nothing, but of resistance,
which mattered much. No fewer than three
menacing letters to Oxford had been needed
before its divines would interpret a point of
canonical law in the sense their king commanded. Such indiscipline seemed to Henry
intolerable. He must take steps to crush
it before he could proceed with Cromwell's

scheme, should that scheme become necessary. He dared not open his main attack upon the Pope while there was risk of mutiny at home. For the present, however, he had no decisive news of the Pope's intentions, although his envoys had reached Italy about the time when Fox and Gardiner were intriguing at Cambridge.

As it chanced, no time could have been less propitious. In February 1530 Wiltshire and Cranmer found the Pope not at Rome, but at Bologna, where he was engaged upon the long-deferred coronation of the emperor. The moment when he was occupied with crowning the nephew of Katharine was hardly the moment for welcoming the father of Anne. Wiltshire's failure was complete. He proposed that the hearing of "the king's matter" should be remitted by the Pope to the Archbishop of Canterbury. Clement refused. Katharine had appealed in due form, and he had already notified his intention of hearing her appeal, jointly with the king's, in Rome. Indeed, Wiltshire's presence as the king's representative removed the only difficulty in the way of that plan. A citation to Henry had been prepared, summoning him to appear in the papal court when Katharine's appeal was heard. But there had been no means of

serving it.   If Clement invited any of his
officials to journey to England and to approach Henry VIII. with such a document,
it is scarcely surprising that the official found
reason to decline.   Now there was a way out
of this dilemma.   The citation was thrust
upon the dismayed Earl of Wiltshire.   Thereupon he abandoned negotiations, and, with
this most unwelcome addition to his luggage,
took ship for England.   The attitude of the
emperor towards the Boleyn family may well
have hastened his departure.

But the proposal he had made has a point
of interest which seems to have escaped
notice.   It proves, we submit, that Cranmer's
elevation to the primacy, so far from being,
as is commonly supposed, an impulsive act
of 1532, was already a part of Henry's policy
in 1530.   Wiltshire urged, at the king's
bidding, that the decision of the case should
be made over by the Pope to the Archbishop
of Canterbury.   The Archbishop at this time
was William Warham.   To remit the hearing
to him, so far from profiting Henry, would
have been to ensure a judgement in Katharine's
favour.   Warham had never been a man of
conspicuous powers, and now was aged and
infirm.   Yet neither lack of power nor the
burden of years could degrade William

F

Warham into becoming the tool of Henry
VIII. From the first he had spoken of the
king's matrimonial designs with abhorrence.
His last public utterance was a condemnation of them, as just as it was courageous.
Not to Warham, then, could the king have
dreamed of entrusting his fortunes. The
Archbishop to whom he would have the case
referred must be a man of another type,
a man who would obey orders, a man who
could be trusted to annul the marriage with
Katharine and approve the marriage with
Anne. Need we ask who was to be this
complacent prelate ? Henry's scheme is
clear. If Wiltshire could gain the decree
for which he applied, it would not be utilised
immediately. Warham was over eighty. He
was seriously ill. At best he might be
persuaded to retire. At worst he must die
before long. Cranmer should succeed him,
and should exercise those powers which the
Pope had been lured into granting, not to
Warham as an individual, but to the Archbishop, in virtue of his office. The Pope,
as we have seen, was not so lured. The
execution of the plan had to be postponed.
But the incident shows that Cranmer's
future, unknown to himself, had already been
decided by his master. It shows also how

far-sighted was Henry VIII., with what fore-
thought he framed his schemes, how effect-
ively he contrived that the impatient ardour
of his heart should not affect the cold working
of his astounding brain. He lost his temper
almost daily, his judgement never.

Cranmer did not return to England with
Wiltshire and the other envoys. He remained in the Pope's company and, when
the business attendant on the coronation
was finished, removed with him to Rome.
He was there throughout the summer. His
letters show that he continued to urge the
king's suit. He did so not merely without
success, but without the slightest chance of
success. Had he addressed himself to show-
ing how the Pope, while satisfying Henry,
could afford to brave the wrath of Charles,
he would have had an eager hearing. The
Pope made no pretence of viewing the
question as one of abstract principle. He
and his cardinals were practical politicians.
They would have conceded with alacrity
whatever the king asked, knowing the importance of his friendship, if only they could
escape the immediate wrath of the offended
emperor. They were not impressed when
Cranmer plied them with impersonal points
of canon law as though he were maintaining

a thesis in his Cambridge lecture-room. Clement may have been amused by the guilelessness of a man who could labour such arguments before such an audience. At least he was notably gracious to Cranmer, kept him as his guest, and appointed him Grand Penitentiary, an office of nominal duties. So the months slipped by. We may suppose that Cranmer spent much of his leisure happily enough among the treasures of the Vatican library. At last, in September 1530, he returned to England.

Here the king was about to make the next move in his game. Wolsey died in November. Two months later the archaic weapon which had been used to crush him was brought out again to bludgeon the whole English Church into submission. Wolsey had held the office of Pope's legate. Thereby, Henry claimed, he had broken the *praemunire* Act of 1393. That he had become legate with the king's express consent, that he had used his legatine powers in the king's service, were irrelevant details. In accordance with the vague yet comprehensive wording of the statute, the whole of the Cardinal's vast possessions were adjudged by the king himself to be forfeit to the crown. After Wolsey's death the king professed to have made a further discovery.

All the bishops and clergy had recognised Wolsey as legate. Therefore all the bishops and clergy had shared Wolsey's guilt, had violated the Act of 1393, and were liable to the penalties of a *praemunire*. Yet the king would be graciously pleased to pardon them, on certain conditions. Convocation must acknowledge that he was " sole protector and Supreme Head of the Church and clergy of England ". The province of Canterbury must pay him £100,000 by way of fine ; the province of York, £18,840. Then Parliament was instructed to pass Acts embodying these financial terms. The Canterbury measure was careful to explain that " his Highness, having alway tender eye with mercy and pity towards his said spiritual subjects . . . of his mere motion, benignity, and liberality hath given and granted his liberal and free pardon to his said good and loving spiritual subjects ".

The Commons did not pass this extraordinary measure without demur. It suggested vividly the danger of their own position. The king had used this weapon of *praemunire* against Wolsey. He had used it against the clergy. There seemed every likelihood that the laity might be its next victims. They were in the same case as the others, having recognised the legatine status of the Cardinal. That the king himself had done so would not protect them. At the not remote time when he would have squandered all Wolsey's fortune and exhausted the £118,000 he had stolen from the Church, it would be strange if the laity were not forced by the same expedient to satisfy his greed. Therefore they took care to protect themselves in good season. They demanded, and secured, an Act of indemnity for themselves as the condition of their passing the Act for the pardon of the clergy.

Henry had no reason to resist this, for he had achieved his real purpose. He had made his power felt. He had brought the Church to heel. He had compelled the admission of his supremacy. Moreover, the Church was under no illusion of security by reason of its purchased " pardon ". The provisions of the archaic statute were far-reaching. Transactions with Rome were a necessary part of ecclesiastical business. Any one of these transactions, if the king so chose, might be construed as an infringement of the law. With this threat hanging over it, the spirit of the Church was broken. Henceforth it was afraid to make any articulate protest against Henry's schemes. These might be highly unpopular. They might violate the laws of religion and defy every canon of decency. They might modify the whole social life of the nation. Not improbably they would plunge England into war. At the same time they might effect some useful reforms and terminate alien interference with English affairs. But, good or evil, popular or unpopular, Henry was now, as he had planned, in a position to push them forward. A packed Parliament would execute his wishes, and a gagged Church would raise no protest against them.

Cranmer probably remained in England through the spring and early summer of 1531, but we have no record of him before June 13. On that day he was at Hampton Court, the splendid palace which the king had confiscated from Wolsey. On that day he addressed a long letter to " the Right Honourable, and my singular good Lord, my Lord of Wiltshire ". Its main purpose was to describe a book written by Reginald Pole on the marriage question : " the principal intent whereof is that the king his grace should be content to commit his great cause to the judgment of the Pope ; wherein meseemeth he lacketh much judgment. But he suadeth that with such goodly eloquence that he were like to persuade many." Cranmer then gives, with remarkable fairness, a summary of Pole's arguments. It is evident that they had made a great impression upon him, and he concedes to Pole's writing such charm " that if it were set forth and known to the common people, I suppose it were not possible to persuade them to the contrary ". But the most significant, and the most sinister, sentence of this letter to Anne Boleyn's father occurs near its close. " The king and my lady Anne rode yesterday to Windsor, and this night they be looked for again at Hampton Court ; God be their guide." Henry's marriage with Katharine had not been annulled. It was upon a pair living, to the scandal of a court far from strait-laced, in open adultery that Cranmer piously invoked the Divine blessing.

Within a short time of writing this letter, Cranmer was sent by the king to Germany. In name, he was ambassador to Charles V. In fact, his mission was to discuss "the king's matter " with German princes, universities, and divines, in order to bring them to a right way of thinking. He took pains also to note the conditions of the provinces through which he travelled, to remark their trade, their armaments, their politics, and to convey his observations to the king. With such miscellaneous information two extant despatches of his are filled. With special interest he records the appearance of " a blazing star, called *cometa* ". It is difficult to find in them anything that could have been of practical value to the King of England. Probably, however, Henry's chief motive for sending Cranmer to Germany was to place him for a time in a definitely anti-papal atmosphere. The king was about to break with the Pope. Cranmer was about to become Archbishop. It was of importance, therefore, that the future Archbishop should be purged of any papal sympathies. If he had shown little sign of them, he was easily impressionable, and in Rome had been on terms of personal friendship with Clement. A sojourn in Germany would supply a corrective. Possibly it had this result, but certainly it turned Cranmer's religious beliefs in the direction of Protestantism. He spent much time with Lutheran teachers. The friendships he made and the doctrines with which he was brought into touch had a permanent influence upon the rest of his life.

Another enduring consequence befell Cranmer as the result of his German visit. He made a second marriage at the age of forty - three, his bride being the young daughter of Andrew Osiander, Lutheran pastor of Nuremberg. This wife bore him two daughters and a son, outlived him, and was twice remarried subsequently. His marriage as a priest transgressed canonical law, yet the law was virtually repealed in Germany and commonly disregarded in England. For an archbishop, however, this uncanonical feature of his household was a considerable embarrassment. The fact that Cranmer married at this date proves that he had no idea of his imminent promotion. His experience with " Black Joan " would have deterred him from a wilful repetition of that blunder. As it was, Margaret Cranmer had to play but a fitful and inconspicuous part in his life. At times when the rule of clerical celibacy was laxly observed or definitely abrogated, she was permitted to live in England. At times when the rule of clerical celibacy was strictly enforced, she was shipped back to Germany. There is no mention of her in the collection of Cranmer's letters, above three hundred in number, which has come down to us. No doubt most of this correspondence is of an official character. References are found in it, however, to his married sister, his brother-in-law, his nephew, and many kinsfolk. But of his wife there is not a word.

While Cranmer was enriching his mind and losing his heart in Germany, in England the king pursued his parliamentary campaign. An Act compelling " the submission of the clergy " silenced Convocation, and took from the English Church the right of making its own rules for its own conduct. The first Annates Act, also passed in 1532, prohibited the payment of the accustomed first-fruits, dues, and fees to Rome. For the present, however, this was cast in a permissive form. It was a weapon the threatened use of which, in Henry's judgement, might make its actual use unnecessary.

At the end of August the aged and courageous Archbishop passed away. In November, Cranmer received a message of recall, intimating that the king had chosen him as Warham's successor. " I protest ", he said in later years to his accusers, " there was never man came more unwillingly to a bishopric than I did to that." The truthfulness of this statement seems beyond question. This amiable scholar wished himself back in Cambridge. Of personal ambition he had no trace. And even a man of strong ambition might have hesitated. He might have paused to count the cost if he realised the Church's position, if he had known by experience the temper of Henry, if he had witnessed the tragedy of Wolsey's end, if he had seen how swift could be the passage from high ecclesiastical office in the king's unbounded favour to overthrow, ignominy, and death.

Slowly and reluctantly Cranmer journeyed to England. In after years he declared that " when king Henry did send for me, I prolonged my journey by seven weeks at least, thinking that he would be forgetful of me in the meantime ". This proved, assuming the motive named to be real, how imperfect as yet was his acquaintance with Henry's character. Not in seven, or seventy, weeks was his tenacious mind likely to forget a tool he had made ready for his purpose. If he sent no peremptory message to hasten Cranmer on his way, that was because the consecration as Archbishop was not yet practicable. Papal bulls to sanction it had first to be obtained. The new Archbishop would soon have to play the final part in the marriage business. No question must then be raised of his valid consecration. In order that he might securely defy the Pope he must first be blessed by the Pope. Yet the bulls were not easy to obtain, for relations with Rome were already near breaking-point. It was doubtful if the package sent would contain the bull for Cranmer's consecration or the sentence of Henry's excommunication. At this point the Annates Act of the previous year was turned to good account. The Pope and his cardinals were informed that the operation of the Act would be no longer suspended unless the bulls were forthcoming. The threat prevailed, and the bulls, in due form, were sent. They came none too soon. Anne, with whom Henry had made a secret marriage, was now known to be with child. Therefore the annulment of the marriage with Katharine and the recognition of the marriage with Anne must be pushed through without delay, in order that Anne's child, and not Katharine's, might become the legitimate heir to the throne of England.

One further difficulty remained. In accordance with ancient usage, and in conformity with the wording of the bulls, Cranmer was required to take an oath of obedience to the see of Rome. Remembering the terrors of the *praemunire* statute, he demurred. But the king was obdurate. For a few weeks longer there must be no open breach with Rome. When the marriage business was complete and an Act forbidding appeals to Rome on the statute-book, the Pope might launch what excommunications he pleased. Until then a semblance of friendship must be preserved. At length Cranmer solved the problem for himself, in a manner as disingenuous as it was characteristic. On the Book of the Holy Gospels he swore to be true and obedient to the see of Peter, to Clement VII. and his successors, to uphold their rights against all men. Also, he made a declaration before a notary that he regarded the oath as a mere matter of form, which he would not consider binding at any point where it conflicted with the wishes of the king.

Thus on March 30, 1533, Thomas Cranmer was duly consecrated as Archbishop of Canterbury, and sat uneasily in the chair of Augustine.

CHAPTER IV

THE KING AND THE CHURCH

THE story of Cranmer's primacy will be more intelligible if we can discern at its outset the principles which shaped his conduct. Few characters have been estimated more variously than his. Some historians have attempted to canonise him as a leader of the Reformation. Passing lightly over ignoble details of his life, they have preferred to emphasise its dramatic ending. He was burned by the Romanists. Consequently, he was a martyr. And it follows, in their view, that he who died as a martyr must have lived as a saint. At the other extreme are writers who attack Cranmer as a mere time-serving politician. His religion, they declare, was a pretence. His creed assumed at any moment whatever colour political expediency might suggest. He had no strong convictions of his own, but was a skilful advocate of any case, good or bad, which he was required to support.

An impartial survey justifies neither of these verdicts. Cranmer's religious writings and devotions are such as no hypocrite could have penned. It is true that they lack the passionate ardour shown, in opposite schools of thought, by such men as Fisher and Latimer. Cranmer's religion was somewhat academic, frigid, devoid of emotion. Yet its reality is beyond question. His piety and habits of prayer, if they were untinged by passion, were untainted by pretence.

Yet, sincerely religious as he was, he did many things which can only be described as infamous. Endeavours to justify them are attempts to defend the indefensible. The plea has been raised that they are not to be judged by modern standards, and that, reprehensible as they must seem to us, they did not offend the moral sense of his own age. No plea could be less fortunate, for this is precisely what they did. Crowds in the London streets protested against immorality at which Cranmer had readily connived. Ploughmen in the villages took up arms to defend Church property which Cranmer had surrendered without a struggle. Many a toping squire, many a wool-merchant who cheated his customers on market-day, would have thought scorn to treat a wronged and defenceless woman as this cultured and devout Archbishop treated Katharine. Many a humble priest would have given his life to save the Church from wrongs which its Primate raised not a finger to avert. Few good men have done so many bad things. Perhaps the English Church has never had an archbishop at once so amiable and so incompetent.

The clue to these discrepancies, however, is evident. It lies partly in the general weakness of Cranmer's character, but more particularly in his abject subservience to despotism. Other men accepted in theory the divine right of kings ; no other made it in the same degree the controlling principle of his life. The king, in his view, could do no wrong. He was the source of all authority, ecclesiastical as well as civil. The king could consecrate or ordain independently of the episcopate. The Church existed to be his instrument. The whole duty of an archbishop was to be his executive officer. Not merely the institutions but the formularies of the Church must be modified as the king thought fit. Doctrine was true or false as he decided. In the succeeding century another archbishop was to uphold the divine right of kings. But we can imagine Laud's reply had he been told that every doctrinal utterance of his as Primate must be subject to revision by Charles I. Such, however, was the attitude of Cranmer to Henry VIII. Having framed a statement of his sacramental beliefs, he appended the characteristic and remarkable words : " This is my opinion and sentence at present, which nevertheless I do not temerariously define, but refer the judgment thereof wholly to your Majesty." He could not have shown more vividly how unstable was his creed, how unconditional his subservience to the king. Moreover, he held that the ecclesiastical supremacy of the crown could be delegated at pleasure. If the monarch chose to invest with his authority a Cromwell or a Somerset, then to Cromwell or Somerset the same unquestioning obedience must be paid as to Henry VIII. or Edward VI. Such were the principles which governed Cranmer's conduct. They account for actions of his which, apart from them, must seem inexplicable. One further point is to be noted. To his belief that the king could do no wrong he added, after a while, an equally fixed conviction that the Pope could do no right. It was the conjunction of these ideas which brought about the final dilemma of his life, when a monarch whom it was his duty to obey required submission to a Pope whom it was his duty to defy.

With these facts before us we can resume our study of his career.

Having been appointed Primate, he had quickly to complete the task which was the cause of his appointment. Convocation, despite a courageous protest from Fisher, had already expressed the opinion on the marriage question which the king demanded. But Henry wished to pretend that Cranmer acted on his own initiative in taking the final steps. He had been consecrated on March 30, 1533. On April 11, being Good Friday, he had to petition for leave to decide the king's cause. Two drafts of his letter survive. Their language, and that of the king's reply, is both odious and significant. It shows how complete was to be the subjection of the spiritual leader to the crown under Henry's scheme of government; it shows also how readily Cranmer acquiesced in this degradation of his office. " Prostrate at the feet of your Majesty ", the Archbishop, " though a poor wretch and much unworthy ", craves leave to " proceed to the examination, final determination and judgment in the great cause touching your Highness ". He asks this, as " it shall not become me, forasmuch as your Grace is my prince and sovereign, to enterprise any part of my office in the said weighty cause touching your Highness, without your Grace's favour and licence obtained in that behalf ".

The king is benevolently pleased to grant the petition. Indeed, he " cannot but commend and laud your good and virtuous purpose. In consideration whereof, albeit we, being your king and sovereign, do recognise no superior in earth, but only God, and not being subject to the laws of any other earthly creature, yet because ye be under us, by God's calling and ours, the most principal minister of our spiritual jurisdiction . . . we will not therefore refuse your humble request to mean to make an end, according to the will and pleasure of Almighty God, in our said great cause of matrimony, which hath so long depended and undetermined, to our great and grievous inquietness and burthen of our conscience."

The sordid farce was played to its end. On May 11 Cranmer held his court in Dunstable Priory. It stood within four miles of Ampthill, where at this time Katharine was virtually a prisoner. Moreover, it was conveniently remote from public observation.

As Katharine did not appear, she was adjudged contumacious. On May 17 Cranmer wrote to Cromwell, beseeching him to keep the proceedings secret, for if " the Lady Katharine be counselled or persuaded to appear before me, I shall be thereby greatly stayed in the process ". To his relief, she treated his court with scorn. He was able to carry through the proceedings without having to face her righteous indignation. On May 23 he gave formal sentence that her marriage with Henry VIII. was invalid and null. On the same day she, who had been Queen for twenty-four years, was commanded to abandon the title. Five days later the Archbishop held another secret court at Lambeth, and, without a shred of evidence, pronounced the marriage with Anne Boleyn to be lawful. On June 1 he crowned Anne. The people of London showed their feelings by refusing to uncover as she passed. In September Elizabeth was born, whom Mary, the daughter of Katharine, was compelled to serve as maid. Only after long delay did the Pope give judgment in favour of Katharine and excommunicate Henry. His belated action had been foreseen and neutralised by anti-papal statutes which Henry had forced through Parliament. Through the next three years Katharine was acclaimed at every opportunity by the people and persecuted at every turn by the king. In 1536 she died. Henry and Anne welcomed the news of her passing by donning bright clothes and holding revels at Court. Such was the end of a tragic and stainless life ; such the conclusion of an episode in which Cranmer, if the mere tool of a despot, played a conspicuous and ignoble part.

For eighteen months after Anne's coronation Cranmer was allowed to be Archbishop in fact as well as in name. Through the following five years his primatial powers were to be virtually transferred to the unscrupulous hands of Cromwell. In the meantime, however, he was able to work more or less as he chose, provided that his choice did not run counter to Henry's wishes. He planned a task of considerable magnitude. He resolved to hold a provincial visitation ; to visit officially, that is, each diocese within his province of Canterbury, and to inhibit the diocesan bishops from visiting until his own survey had been completed. Three reasons very probably may have led him to this enterprise. In the first place, he was anxious to show his zeal, to assert his prerogative, and to justify his appointment. In the second place, it was desirable to come into direct contact with his clergy, and to persuade them, if he could, that his actions at the king's bidding had not deserved their censure. For that censure they had emphatically received. Up and down the country the clergy were risking remarks about the king and applying the frankest scriptural terms to Anne. Indeed, Cranmer had found it necessary for a time to prohibit all preaching in his own diocese, and to permit it only under stringent conditions elsewhere. As for his repute among his brethren of the Church, he confessed to Audeley, the Lord Chancellor, that " of all sorts of men I am daily informed that the priests report the worst of me ". A visitation, with its personal intercourse, might help to better this opinion.

One further reason may have influenced Cranmer. The labours of a provincial visitation must be arduous. As their records testify, the proceedings of a visitation were neither rapid nor formal. They involved tedious sittings, with minute investigation of details. And for the Archbishop a provincial visitation must mean long days in the saddle, with all the dangers and discomforts that travel in the sixteenth century entailed. Yet, if such a visitation was laborious, it was also exceedingly lucrative. Heavy fees were exacted from the places visited. Cranmer was in urgent need of money. In the year of his consecration he acknowledges a gift from the monks of Christ Church, Canterbury, but adds : " nevertheless you should have done me much more greater pleasure if you had lent it me full of gold " ; not for his own enjoyment, he explains, but to satisfy troublesome creditors. Therefore he begs the prior and brethren to grant him a loan. In the same year he tries through Cromwell to obtain a loan of £660 from the king, but the king will not advance more than £500. In such circumstances, his share of the visitation fees would be exceedingly useful.

Chiefly, no doubt, because an archbishop's official visit was a costly honour to the visited, the news of Cranmer's project proved far from welcome. The Bishops of Winchester and of London went to the length of addressing formal protests against it to the king. It is true that personal jealousy may have had some part in their action. Gardiner had been head of a house at Cambridge when Cranmer was a mere tutor. From this time to the end he was to prove the Archbishop's bitterest foe ; though in justice it must be added that his hatred of Cranmer was not more emphatic or outspoken than Cranmer's hatred of Gardiner. As for Stokesley, Bishop of London, he had acted as Warham's deputy during the last years of that venerable Primate, and probably had expected to succeed him. Gardiner represented that his diocese had borne the expense of a visitation by Warham but five years previously. Stokesley relied chiefly on the point that earlier primates had visited not as archbishops but in virtue of their authority as papal legates, an office now extinct in England. But Cranmer had been prudent enough to obtain in advance the king's consent for the visitation he proposed. Gardiner and Stokesley protested in vain. Yet time soon brought them revenge. They must have been vastly pleased when, within two years, Cranmer's own visitatorial powers were suspended, and, so far from being free to exercise this function throughout his province, he dared not visit officially even his diocese of Canterbury until he had obtained the written consent of Thomas Cromwell.

An interesting example of Cranmer's method survives in the account of his visit to the Benedictine priory of Worcester. Its prior's journal for 1534 records that " My Lord of Canterbury came to Worcester Friday night, and visited in his own person

Monday, the 17th of August, Tuesday, Wednesday, and Thursday ". These four days devoted to investigation show that the Archbishop did his work with painstaking thoroughness. For some unexplained reason the " injunctions " based upon the results were not despatched by Cranmer until six months later. They are dated February 22. Yet the fact that this long interval was permitted may be taken to prove that no wrong was discovered which called for prompt action. The injunctions are thirteen in number. The first orders that " a lecture on Holy Scripture shall be delivered for the space of one hour before noon, in some place suitable thereto within your monastery, and that it be expounded and interpreted, at least as to its literal sense, plainly and intelligibly ". The second regulates the use of the monastery's common seal, the third orders an inventory of goods to be kept, the fourth that the accounts be published to the whole monastery. The fifth requires that " a man of good character and sufficiently learned in the knowledge of grammar " shall be employed to teach the younger monks. The remaining injunctions are concerned with such details as the provision of " wholesome and well-cooked food, especially for those who dine in the refectory ", and of " suitable

lights in the refectory ". Another enjoins
that the prior must not be " cruel or austere ".

This, when we remember the man who
framed it and the date—within five years of
the suppression—at which it was framed,
must seem a striking document, remarkable
for its statements and even more remarkable
for its implications. It shows the high value
attached by Cranmer to an intelligent knowledge of Scripture. His zeal for this knowledge and his consistent efforts to promote it
are among the most laudable points of his
career. But what the document does not say
is more important than what it says. Cranmer
has no quarrel with the monastic system.
Three years later the same house was visited
by Latimer, who as a matter of course
vehemently assailed the " ignorance and
negligence " of its inmates, " for that thereby
doth reign idolatry and many kinds of super-
stition and other enormities ". The Worcester
ritual, in other words, was not such as Latimer
could approve. But Cranmer finds nothing
to amend in it, nor any superstitious usage to
denounce. He has no charge of vice, indo-
lence, or scandalous conversation to bring.
The prior must not bully. The refectorer
must be less niggardly with his candles, the
cook more careful with his cooking. If, after

four days of searching enquiry, such were the worst faults that could be found to need correction, it does not seem that much was amiss with the priory of Worcester.

While the Archbishop was occupied in this way, the king was strenuously engaged in consolidating his position. What he had brought to pass was not merely a series of changes but a revolution. The whole relations of king, Church, and people were transformed. An autocracy such as England had never known was set up. Customs, laws, and institutions that had endured through centuries were swept away in a few months. Now the new order had to be firmly established, and the risk of counter-revolution forestalled. That the risk was far from negligible Henry knew well. Abroad he had made the Pope and the emperor his enemies. At home his proceedings had been odious to most of his subjects and particularly offensive to the Church. He had angered the merchants by a foreign policy which hampered their lucrative trade with Flanders. Invasion was possible, and people were heard to whisper that if Charles landed with an army they would not support Henry against him. There was a greater likelihood of risings at home. Disaffected groups in the provinces seemed only to need a common leader in order to break into revolt. So uncertain was the mood of London that guns were mounted in the Tower to menace the city.

In these circumstances the king's policy was simple and characteristic. He would continue on the course he had planned. So far from abating any of his claims, he would establish them more firmly. He would compel Parliament to confirm explicitly every right he had devised for himself, to destroy the last vestige of papal authority, to approve not merely his morals and theology but his supremacy as a theologian and a moralist, and to ensure the succession of his heir by Anne Boleyn. Then he would enforce upon individual subjects by oath that belief in his infallibility which had been set forth by statute. This would be a serviceable test. They who refused would show themselves traitors, and with traitors he knew how to deal. Finally, he would punish the recalcitrant Church by confiscating its vast possessions, using part for his personal enrichment and the remainder for judicious bribery. By these steps his absolute rule over Church and State would be embodied in the laws of England, rebels would be detected and dealt with ruthlessly, criticism would be terrorised into silence, and some of the popular support he had forfeited would be regained by astute purchase.

Such was the policy framed by the king in collaboration with Cromwell, now his chief agent and counsellor. Each stage of it was carried through with unfaltering precision. It may seem strange that Parliament should have been willing to play the part assigned to it. Yet loyalty to the crown, despite the strain imposed by Henry's conduct, was still a tradition too strong to be easily broken. Again, dislike of papal interference was sufficiently general to ensure the passage of anti-papal legislation. But Henry and Cromwell did not rely only on such facts as these. They left nothing to chance. Having selected the tasks Parliament was to perform, they selected the Parliament to perform them. Spiritual peers whose attitude was doubtful were warned to absent themselves. The House of Commons was sedulously packed. A suggestive example may be cited. On May 12, 1536, the Sheriff of Canterbury reports to Cromwell that the electors were assembled on the previous day and unanimously chose John Starkey, alderman, and Christopher Levyns, common clerk, as their representatives. After the election the writer had been shown a letter from Cromwell desiring that John Briggs and Robert Darknall should be chosen. He regrets that the letter reached him too late. On May 18 Cromwell writes to the magistrates of Canterbury. He reminds them that " the King's pleasure and commandment is that Robert Darknall and John Briggs should be elect and chosen. But ye have chosen other at your own wills and minds, contrary to the king's pleasure and commandment in that behalf, whereat the king's highness doth not a little marvel. Wherefore, in avoiding of further displeasure that might thereby ensue, I require you on the king's behalf that, notwithstanding the said election, ye proceed to a new, and elect these other, without failing to do so, as ye intend to avoid his highness's displeasure at your peril." Within two days the Mayor and Corporation of Canterbury are able to inform Cromwell that this has been done. Having received his letter, immediately they summoned the electors anew, when Darknall and Briggs were elected " freely, with one voice, and without contradiction ".

This example of a " free " election is illuminating. Certain writers have argued that Henry's policy must have been welcome to the English people, since it was readily supported by the English Parliament. The Canterbury incident reveals how that support was obtained and how far it represented the unconstrained wishes of the electorate. Henry's absolutism was complete. It was he who decided what Parliament should do, when it should sit, and who should sit in Parliament.

In the first three months of 1534 a series of stringent anti-papal measures became law. Among them was a new Annates Act, which confirmed that method of electing bishops which is still in use. The dean and chapter were to receive from the crown a licence to elect, together with a letter missive nominating the person who, under penalty of a *praemunire*, was to be elected. The same Act embodies a remarkable instance of the king's audacity. Only two years earlier an Act had abolished the payment of first-fruits, on the plea that they were an " intolerable burden ", based on " no just or good title ", and that the realm was " impoverished " by such exactions. Now Henry proposed to revive these payments, with the single difference that they were to be made to himself instead of to the Pope. Considering the language of the earlier Act, this might seem difficult. But the preamble of the new Act

easily overcame the difficulty. It is too long
to be quoted in full, yet too humorous to be
omitted entirely. It begins :

Forasmuch as it is and of very duty ought to be
the natural inclination of all good people, like most
faithful, loving, and obedient subjects, sincerely and
willingly to provide not only for the public weal of
their native country but also for the supportation,
maintenance, and defence of the royal estate of their
most dread, benign, and gracious Sovereign Lord,
upon whom and in whom dependeth all their joy
and wealth, in whom also is united and knit so
princely a heart and courage, mixed with wisdom,
mercy, and justice, and also a natural affection
joined to the same. . . .

It proceeds to allege that the Lords and
Commons, " calling to remembrance not
only the manifold and innumerable benefits
daily administered by his Highness to them
all ", but also " what great, excessive, and
inestimable charges his Highness hath hitherto
been at ", humbly implore him to confiscate
a portion of clerical incomes for his own use.
Probably Cranmer absented himself from
the House of Lords when this preposterous
measure was brought forward. Certainly he
did not venture to oppose it.

The anti-papal measures were rounded off
in 1536 by an Act " for the extirpation,
abolition, and extinguishment out of this
realm of the pretended power and usurped

H

authority of the Bishop of Rome, by some
called the Pope ". One part of Henry's
scheme was now complete. Meanwhile, he
had pressed forward another. He had resolved to suppress by violence every opinion
which differed from his own, and to keep his
" most faithful, loving, and obedient subjects"
from revolt by establishing a reign of terror.
His first victim was Elizabeth Barton, a nun
of St. Sepulchre's, Canterbury. Devotion,
deceit, and delusion seem all to have had
a place in her strange personality. So long
as she merely professed to receive divine
messages in general, she was regarded as
harmless, and indeed was patronised as a
soothsayer by numbers of eminent people.
But in an unhappy moment she began to give
her visions a political colour. Her revelations included a lurid forecast of the doom
awaiting Henry as recompense for his treatment of Katharine. She was brought in
custody to Cranmer, who played a not very
creditable part in her examination. She
was then placed in the Tower, where she
signed a confession of deceit. Had the king
been content to publish her confession, to see
her expelled from her convent, and even to
punish her with a term of imprisonment, he
would have taken a course both legitimate

and adequate. This would not content him. He was determined to make an example. England must know how he would deal with any who aspersed his marriage with Anne. As no statute yet in force was sufficient for his purpose, a special bill of attainder was passed. Elizabeth Barton was executed for high treason.

Whatever its effect elsewhere, this event caused the monks of Christ Church, Canterbury, as Cranmer found, " great pensiveness and dolour ". It was not surprising, for two members of their house had been closely associated with Elizabeth Barton and had shared her fate. It seemed likely enough that Henry would turn upon the others. Therefore the Archbishop sent a very judicious letter on their behalf. He described them as most " conformable and reformable ". He assured the king that none but a few novices had given any credence to the nun's revelations. All the brethren were " discomforted, dismayed, and sad ". If the king would show them his favour, they would pray that his noble estate might long and prosperously endure. Also (an argument which not impossibly had more force with Henry) they would " offer unto your Grace for a pleasure two or three hundred pounds ".[1]   On these terms the king was content to leave them in peace for a few years.

The Acts of Supremacy and Succession, the oath requiring their complete acceptance, and the Verbal Treasons Act equipped the king with all the weapons he needed. Their ruthless use soon followed. In May 1535 four Carthusian monks were butchered with every circumstance of revolting barbarity. Other undistinguished victims were sent to the stake. But all Christendom quivered with horrified indignation when Henry's insensate fury refused to spare Bishop Fisher and Sir Thomas More. Both were deeply loved and revered. We have spoken in an earlier chapter of Fisher's place in the University of Cambridge. Now in his sixty-seventh year, he was still its Chancellor. None had fostered the advancement of learning with more zeal or with greater visible result. Cambridge was aghast at the news of his danger. St. John's College, which he had befriended from its birth, sent him a letter in his day of trouble ; a letter phrased in official Latin, yet so simply genuine in its sorrow, gratitude, affection, and pathetic

---

[1] The equivalent of at least £2000 or £3000 in modern money.

eagerness to help that even now it cannot be read without emotion. No one knew better than Cranmer what place was filled by its Chancellor in the life of Cambridge. As a bishop he had proved sagacious and tolerant. But, if Fisher is to be placed among the greatest men of his own age, Sir Thomas More must be admitted to rank among the greatest Englishmen of any age. Seldom have gifts so various been united in one person. His profound learning was matched by his simplicity. His wisdom was irradiated by wit. His writings are among the permanent treasures of English literature. His exquisite serenity of temper, which neither reverses of fortune nor the malice of enemies could perturb, was based upon an inner life of intense piety and devotion. Such was the man whom Henry in bygone years had used as a familiar friend. Such was the man now doomed by Henry to a traitor's death.

For a time Fisher and More lay sentenced to perpetual imprisonment. Then they were told that they must swear to the new statutes or die. They were willing to accept the Act of Succession, to serve Henry loyally as king, to recognise Anne Boleyn's child as his heir. They were not willing to swear that any lay person had the right to style himself Supreme Head of the Church. They were not willing to swear that Henry's marriage with Katharine had been invalid. But nothing less would placate the king. Cranmer, though afraid to approach the king himself, pleaded with Cromwell that acceptance of the Act of Succession might be allowed to suffice, " and peradventure it should be a good quietation to many others within this realm ". The plea was vain. The king warned Cranmer, through Cromwell, not to repeat his argument. If More and Fisher, known at heart to disallow the Supreme Headship, were allowed to live, encouragement might be given to others with secret leanings to that opinion. No hint of dissent from the royal doctrine could be tolerated. Moreover, at this stage an untoward incident fanned the king's fury afresh. Clement's successor, Pope Paul III., proposed to appoint seven new cardinals, and included Fisher in the list. Henry swore that when the cardinal's hat reached England, there should be no head to wear it. Fisher must die, and More, sharing his views, must share his fate. On June 22, 1535, Bishop Fisher was beheaded on Tower Hill. Fourteen days later Sir Thomas More followed him to the block.

To this tragedy, horrifying not merely England but Europe, Cranmer makes no reference in his letters. At least it did not shake his faith in the king. He showed his devotion to the royal cause by apprehending and sending in custody to Cromwell men and women who had spoken well of the Pope or slightingly of the queen. Over a long period he seems to have had no personal touch with the king. The chief event of 1536, which caused little surprise to those at court, came as a staggering blow to the Archbishop.

Henry had wearied quickly of Anne. He had indeed been unfaithful to her within a few weeks of her wedding. After various affairs with various ladies, he had become enamoured of Jane Seymour. He knew that Anne was detested by the people, and she had not borne him the male child he desired to ensure the succession. Then, most opportunely from the king's point of view, occurred the death of Katharine. When Anne danced with Henry to celebrate the news, she little guessed that it brought her own death-warrant. Now that Katharine was dead, Henry saw that, with Anne out of the way, he would be free to make a marriage the validity of which could not be questioned.

For some months he pondered this plan.
His intentions were freely whispered about
the court.   At length his passion for Jane
Seymour impelled him to act ; some indis-
creet words spoken by Anne gave him his
opportunity.   On May 1, 1536, Anne was in
his company as usual.   On the 2nd she was
committed to the Tower, together with her
brother Lord Rochford and four others,
charged with incest and adultery.

On the same day Cranmer, who was in the
country, received a peremptory summons
from the king.   He was to repair at once to
Lambeth and not to quit his house without
leave.   Henry had no wish to answer in-
convenient questions, nor did he mean that
the Archbishop should learn those facts
which any courtier might have told him.
On the next day Cranmer, forbidden as yet
to see the king, wrote him a characteristic
letter.   It must have given the king considerable amusement.   The guileless Primate
likens the sufferings of Henry to those of
Job, and exhorts him not to be crushed by
the terrible calamity that has befallen him.
" I can do no less than most humbly to desire your Grace, by your great wisdom and
the assistance of God's help, somewhat to
suppress the deep sorrows of your Grace's

heart ". For himself, he is " in such a perplexity, that my mind is clean amazed ". Such was his regard for Anne, that he can scarce believe her guilty. Yet, as it is the king who declares her guilty, guilty she must be. Therefore he is bound to " desire the offence without mercy to be punished ". He writes a postscript after receiving more information from the king's messengers. " I am sorry ", he adds, " that such things can be proved by (*i.e.* against) the queen. But I am, and ever shall be, your faithful subject." No two sentences could illustrate more cogently the unswerving attitude of Thomas Cranmer.

On May 15 a court of peers sat for Anne's trial, with that of Rochford. Her supposed accomplices had already been condemned. The proceedings were outrageous. No evidence was called for the prosecution. No counsel was heard for the defence. Anne was taxed with having given a courtier a present of money and with having derided the king's taste in clothes. Of the serious charges against her no proof was even attempted. Yet on those charges she was found guilty and condemned to die. On the 16th Cranmer was instructed to obtain a confession from her, not concerning the matters of her trial, but with reference to some unknown event before her marriage. On the 17th Cranmer held a court and declared, again without producing any evidence, that her marriage had been void from the first. Three years earlier the same Archbishop had held a court and, then also producing no evidence, had pronounced her marriage valid. He had decided previously that the marriage with Katharine was null. Therefore he now maintained that Henry had never been married to Katharine, had never been married to Anne, and consequently was still a bachelor. The king's reason for giving Cranmer such instructions was evident. He wished to say that the unhappy woman who mounted the scaffold was not his wife. It may be remarked that if Anne, as Cranmer decided, had never been wed, she could not have committed adultery, and for adultery she was condemned to die. With logic of that kind, however, Henry had no concern. On May 19 Anne was beheaded. That very day the pliable Archbishop issued a licence for Henry's marriage with Jane Seymour. On the 30th the marriage took place.

Convocation was summoned to approve the action of Cranmer, and obeyed. Parliament was summoned to approve the actions of Cranmer and Convocation, and obeyed. On June 30 it passed a new Succession Act, thanking the king for his latest marriage, pronouncing Elizabeth, like Mary, to be illegitimate, and transferring to Jane Seymour all the rights that previously had been assigned to Anne Boleyn. To such complete subjugation of Church and State had the tyranny of Henry VIII. attained.

Of Cranmer's shameful part in this shameful business little needs to be said. We must make allowance for his natural weakness. We must recognise his extreme gullibility. We must own that certainly his tenure of office, and probably his tenure of life, would have been over from the day when he dared to resist the tyrant's will. Yet when we contrast the weakness of Cranmer with the constancy to death of Fisher and More, when we remember the injury wrought by it not merely to individuals but to the whole Church whose chief officer he was, we can but regret anew that such a post was held by such a man at such a time. We can but mingle pity for the timid servant of a tyrant king with unfaltering censure of an Archbishop who betrayed his Church.

CHAPTER V

SOCIAL AND RELIGIOUS CHANGE

FEW periods in the history of the English Church are more sombre or more strange than the five years between 1535 and 1540. They were remarkable for the importance of their events and for the unimportance of the Archbishop. Through them Cranmer had to endure a humiliation which to any other holder of his office would have seemed intolerable. The king, having secured the title of Supreme Head, argued that he could delegate his supremacy as he pleased. In January 1535 he nominated Thomas Cromwell as his vicar-general or vicegerent. The act had not even the pretence of parliamentary sanction. It was entirely unconstitutional. The post began and ended with Cromwell's tenure of it. While it lasted, however, his authority in ecclesiastical matters was set above that of the archbishops and bishops. Cranmer had to obey his orders.

The vicar-general was commissioned to visit officially the universities and religious houses. He forbade the bishops to hold any visitations in their own dioceses until his survey had been completed. He claimed the right to preside over Convocation. When unable himself to attend, he sent a deputy, and in the historic assembly of the English Church Cromwell's deputy ousted the Archbishop from his seat. It is not surprising that the bishops were indignant, alike at this intrusion and at the suspension of their work in their own dioceses. Already some doubted the gain of having exchanged the occasional interference of the Pope for the continuous tyranny of the king. Submission to the crown, however, was vastly different from subjection to a man of Cromwell's notorious antecedents and character. To be ruled in spiritual matters by a royal Supreme Head was bad enough. To be bullied by a deputy Supreme Head in this fashion seemed insufferable.

Yet they could make no effective protest when their leader refused to lead. While other prelates chafed at Cromwell's dictatorship, Cranmer acquiesced in it without the slightest demur. If we turn to the very numerous letters addressed to Cromwell by the Archbishop within these five years, in none do we find even a hint of remonstrance, or the faintest wish to assert the spiritual jurisdiction of the Primate. Their tone throughout is one of rather obsequious friendship. They are to be explained, no doubt, by Cranmer's honest adherence to his fixed principle. The king could do no wrong. Cromwell's actions fulfilled the king's desires. Therefore Cromwell's actions must be right. This was fortunate for Cranmer's personal tranquillity, as it made him insensitive to affront. But it was unfortunate for the Church. It caused him to surrender without effort rights that were more than personal ; rights which, as the Church's leader, he beyond all others should have been eager to maintain.

Cromwell's visitation began in the summer of 1535. At Oxford vigorous steps were taken to displace the old learning by the new. Cambridge was supplied with a set of nine " royal injunctions ", mainly directed to the same end. And Cambridge showed its prudence, or its pusillanimity, by electing Cromwell to its chancellorship. University reform, however, was but a minor detail of the task to which Cromwell had addressed himself. Its main purpose was the visitation

and overthrow of the religious houses. Swiftly
and ruthlessly he effected as great a change in
the social life of England as the king already
had brought about in its political system.

The dissolution of the monasteries has
long been the theme of ardent controversy.
A full examination of the evidence would be
beyond the scope of these pages. Yet we
may protect ourselves against an error which
has complicated the debate by confusing
issues entirely distinct. Was the state of the
monasteries satisfactory in 1535 and their
value unimpaired ? Could they have been
left as they were with profit to the life of the
Church and nation ? Such is one of the
enquiries we have to answer. The second
is quite different. Can the actual treatment
which the monasteries received at the hands
of Cromwell and his associates be justified ?
Probably most impartial students will answer
each of these questions with an equally
emphatic negative. All was not well with
the monasteries. The system could not be
allowed to continue without change. Something needed to be done. But nothing could
justify what Cromwell did.

The monastic system had reached its
highest point in this country during the
twelfth and thirteenth centuries. From that

time it deteriorated. We need not pause to scrutinise the reasons in detail. But, speaking generally, the ancient ideals were debased. Worldliness crept into the cloister and chapterhouse. The communities began to be more concerned with the management of estates than with the life of the soul. The strictness of the historic rule was relaxed. In course of time also various tasks passed into other hands which once had been done by the monasteries alone. More schools and colleges came into being. Printing made needless the laborious copying of manuscripts in the cloister. The study of Greek and the fruits of the new learning found little place in the religious houses. In place of the leadership which had been theirs through centuries, they began to be content with an intellectual standard lower than that to be found outside their walls.

Thus, through a variety of causes, the influence of the religious houses had waned. Despite their immense religious and social value in the past, by 1535 they had outlived their usefulness. It was significant that, while many had been closed, not one addition to their number had been founded within the previous half century. Pious benefactors felt that their money could be used to better advantage.   Indeed, an institution which had been formerly of high value to the English Church was now an actual menace to its welfare.   There was chronic ill-feeling between the religious and the secular clergy. Many of the chief monasteries were exempt from episcopal control.   In return for tithes impropriated to them, the monasteries served many of the parish churches.   Thus it came about that a proportion of the parochial clergy were men who recognised the authority of their abbot or prior but not that of the bishop.   The result was to divide the Church against itself.

On the other hand, the indiscriminate charges of evil conduct brought against the religious houses were unfounded.   Instances of gross misbehaviour there were, as among thousands of men and women there were bound to be.   Yet, as a body, the monks were generous to the poor, good landlords, and kindly employers of labour.   But they had abandoned their high ideals and no longer commanded much respect.   Their numbers diminished, and some of the smaller houses were almost empty.   It was in these smaller houses of monks, nuns, and friars that discipline was apt to be most lax and financial difficulties most acute.   They con-

I

stituted a problem with which the Church was bound to deal.

The need of dealing with it had been discerned already by Wolsey. He had obtained leave to suppress forty of these smaller monasteries—of which twenty-four actually were closed—and to transfer their inmates to some of the larger and better-conducted houses. Their revenues were assigned to his new college at Oxford. No doubt Wolsey would have attempted a larger scheme of monastic reform had he not been compelled suddenly to concentrate his attention upon the matter of the king's marriage and the questions of foreign policy which it involved.

It was as an assistant in the business of dissolving religious houses that Cromwell had entered Wolsey's service. Even then his shrewd practical abilities had earned for him some degree of fame, and his treatment of monks and nuns some degree of infamy. This earlier experience no doubt led him now to propose another visitation, on a larger scale, and of a kind more directly profitable to the king. His suggestion was made at an opportune moment. The king's intricate foreign policy, with its many quests for useful alliances, had led him for a time to contemplate negotiations with the princes of North Germany. They, however, were Lutherans, and their distrust of Henry's religious views seemed likely to prove an obstacle. Nothing, indeed, would induce Henry to sympathise with Lutheranism, a creed he held in sincere and consistent abhorrence. But the Lutherans inherited from Luther a hatred of monasticism. If an attack on the English monasteries would help to lull their suspicions and to gain their favour, Henry was entirely ready to make it. Apart, too, from any such contingent result, Cromwell's scheme promised immediate and tangible advantages. The royal exchequer was in its usual need of replenishment. Confiscation of monastic property would augment its resources in a very substantial fashion. Accordingly, Cromwell was bidden to execute his plan. His first visitation was begun in July 1535. Waltham Abbey, the last house to survive, was surrendered to the crown on March 23, 1540. Thus was swept out of existence, within five years, that which had been a most important factor in the social and the religious life of England for upwards of five centuries.

Whatever doubts there may be of the houses visited, there can be none concerning the character of the men who visited them. The assistants employed by Cromwell were a set of unscrupulous ruffians. They professed to have completed their survey in an impossibly brief time. Evidence not discoverable in fact was supplied by their bestial imaginations. Commissions of country gentlemen, appointed subsequently to superintend the actual dissolutions, reported on the same houses in a precisely opposite sense. By Cromwell's emissaries the religious were bullied into signing ready-made confessions. They were bribed, with little success, to inform against one another. They were lured by a promise of larger pensions into surrendering their property at once, before any action had been taken by Parliament.

Parliamentary action, however, soon followed. A measure for the suppression of the smaller houses was passed early in 1536. Thereby some £32,000 was transferred to the king's income. The number of religious houses closed was 376. A packed House of Commons did as Cromwell ordered. In the Upper House the abbots assented to the overthrow of the smaller monasteries, in the hope that their votes would purchase safety for their own more important founda-

tions. They were speedily to be undeceived.
That under Cromwell's original scheme
the smaller houses alone were to have
been attacked seems likely enough. The
Act of 1536 alleges that " manifold sin,
vicious, carnal, and abominable living, is
daily used and committed amongst the little
and small abbeys, priories, and other religious
houses " ; but is careful to distinguish these
houses from the " great solemn monasteries
of this realm wherein, thanks be to God,
religion is right well kept and observed ".
To these greater monasteries it proposes that
the inmates of the dissolved smaller houses
shall be transferred. Yet this tribute had
scarcely been embodied in the law of the land
before, with cynical effrontery, it was disregarded. Almost before the dissolution of
the smaller religious houses had been finished,
a precisely similar attack on the houses where
" religion is right well kept and observed "
was begun. The same charges of gross vice
were formulated, with the same lack of
evidence to support them. As before, confessions were put into the mouths of the
unhappy monks, nuns, and friars which had
been drafted in advance by Cromwell's
secretaries. Some specimens of them survive.
A few sentences will illustrate their style.

They occur in the " confession " attributed to St. Andrew's Priory, Northampton, a house of Cluniac monks. The whole document, of immense prolixity, had to be signed by the prior and twelve brethren. Having recited at length the faults of their " voluptuous and carnal appetites ", it proceeds :

Which our most horrible abominations and execrable persuasions of your Grace's people to detestable errors, and our long covered hypocrisy cloaked with feigned sanctity, we revolving daily and continually pondering in our sorrowful hearts, and thereby perceiving the bottomless gulf of everlasting fire ready to devour us if persisting in this state of living we should depart from this uncertain and transitory life ; constrained by the intolerable anguish of our conscience . . . prostrate at the noble feet of your most royal Majesty, most lamentably do crave of your Highness your most gracious pardon. . . .

After many more pages in this strain the real point is reached, and the monks are represented as saying :

We most humbly beseech your Highness that it might like your Majesty, for the discharging and exonerating us of the most grievous burden of our pained conscience to the imminent peril and danger of our own damnation . . . graciously to accept our free gifts without coercion, persuasion, or procurement of any creature living other than of our voluntary free will, all such possessions, right, title, or interest as we the said Prior and convent hath or ever had or are supposed to have had in your said Monastery of Northampton. . . .

The possessions which the king is humbly entreated to accept are then set forth in detail, and the revolting document ends with a prayer for the king's long life, " with fortunate and prosperous success of all your Grace's honourable and devout proceedings ".

In such language, which is indeed beyond comment, were the religious compelled to address Henry VIII. when surrendering to him their houses, churches, property, and possessions. The abbots of Glastonbury, Reading, and Colchester, who resisted, were hanged. The number of monks and nuns evicted was about 8,000. With them suffered a very large number, computed at 60,000, of men, women, and children who had lived on the monastic estates and had been in the employment of the religious houses. It would be needless to picture in detail the insane work of destruction. Buildings of incomparable beauty were laid low. Manuscripts of priceless worth were used as packing-paper, vestments and altar-cloths cut up, plate melted, and even the ruins of the buildings used as common quarries. A few of the monastic churches survive as cathedrals. A few more still exist, though seldom in a complete form, because local residents combined to purchase them from the spoilers, and, as at Tewkesbury, Romsey, and Great Malvern, they became the parish churches. But the few which escaped help us to measure the loss inflicted by the destruction of the rest, and to realise the injury done to religion and art by Henry VIII.'s " honourable and devout proceedings ".

Enduring social, educational, and economic changes followed the dissolution of the religious houses. On the one hand, it reduced thousands of the labouring class to destitution. On the other, it created a new race of land-owners. Traders were able to acquire monastic properties from the crown. Persons of consequence obtained them as gifts, or, to speak more accurately, as the price for their future support of the king. In fact, a large share of the wealth confiscated from the monasteries was used by Henry to reward his friends and to win over his enemies. Large sums also were retained for his own use, and spent so quickly that four year later he was again requesting Parliament to defray his debts. Under the first proposals for an attack on the monasteries no fewer than twenty-six new bishoprics were to have been endowed from their funds. In practice, this number was reduced to six. Among them was the see of Westminster. After an existence of ten years only, this was abolished, and its income appropriated by the crown.

We must not pause to examine more closely the momentous changes which followed the overthrow of monasticism. Indeed, we should have followed the example of other biographers of Cranmer had we dismissed the whole theme in a sentence, stating casually that the fall of the monasteries took place between 1535 and 1540, but that Cranmer had no part in this event. This is true, yet that it should be true is not less than amazing. It is not a fact to be glossed over in any attempt to estimate Cranmer's character and career. We have seen in brief what happened. A religious institution of vast antiquity was overturned. Hundreds of churches were torn down. Thousands of men and women were defamed and persecuted. More than a million of money was stolen from the Church, a loss the effects of which are felt to this day. These things were done by a greedy and immoral king, an unprincipled minister, and a corrupt parliament. They shook England from one end to the other. They stirred whole counties into active revolt. But they drew not one syllable of protest from the

Archbishop of Canterbury. Cranmer watched the whole proceeding with serene acquiescence. When Cromwell arranged (and the words, in his own handwriting, survive) that two abbots should be " tried and executed," Cranmer remained his close friend. When ancient shrines were stripped of jewels in order that courtiers might adorn their mistresses, the Archbishop had not a word to say. When monastic estates were distributed, he acquired one for himself and endeavoured to obtain another for his nephew. His letter to Cromwell on this matter is remarkable :

My singular good lord, in my most hearty wise I commend me unto your lordship. And whereas I perceive that your lordship, not without urgent and godly considerations, hath suppressed already divers friars' houses, and bestowed them on honest men, as I am informed, which your godly proceeding, as I trust, shall as well extend unto Canterbury as in other places, to the intent that the irreligious religion there may be extincted with other ; and forasmuch as the Gray Friars in Canterbury lieth very commodiously for this bearer, Thomas Cobham . . . these shall be to beseech your lordship to be so good lord unto him as to help him unto the said house of the Gray Friars. . . . Thus, my lord, right heartily fare you well.

It may be added, without much regret, that the request failed. The Gray Friars' house went to another applicant, who doubt-

less outbid Thomas Cobham. But the interest
of the document lies in its disclosure of the
Archbishop's attitude towards the dissolution.
Did he believe that " godly considerations "
governed Cromwell's dealings with the religious houses ? If so, he must have been
almost the one man in England who did not
know Cromwell for the immoral and grasping
adventurer he was.   Again, we must recognise
that Cranmer's religious views, tinged with
Lutheranism, would predispose him to dislike
of monasticism. Had he urged the need of
reform, he would have been amply justified.
Had he attempted to continue the changes
initiated by Wolsey, he would have done the
Church good service.   Had he tried to influence the king and Cromwell, he would have
saved his credit as Archbishop, even had he
tried in vain.   What he did was to watch with
apparent unconcern, or even approval, the
wholesale destruction and confiscation of
Church property, and to ask for a share of the
spoil.

To Cranmer's inaction the records of the
time can supply an effective contrast.   Hugh
Latimer was a Protestant far more extreme
than Cranmer.   His censure of monasticism
was always unbalanced and often unjust.
Yet he discerned the value of its social work,

and foresaw the unhappy results that must follow its cessation. Therefore he had the courage to plead that at least a few monasteries in each county should be spared, and be re-adapted to wider religious and social service. When the Benedictine house of Great Malvern in his diocese was menaced, Latimer wrote to Cromwell on the prior's behalf, asking

for the upstanding of his aforesaid house and continuance of the same to many good purposes— not in monkery, he meaneth not so, God forbid !— but any other ways, as should be thought and seem good to the king's majesty, as to maintain teaching, preaching, study, with praying, and (to which he is much given) good housekeeping, for to the virtue of hospitality he hath been greatly inclined from the beginning, and is very much commended in these parts for the same. . . . He feedeth many, and that daily, for the country is poor and full of penury. And alas, my good lord, shall we not see two or three (*sc.* monasteries) in every shire changed to such remedy ?

The petition failed. The king and Cromwell were little disposed to leave two or three monasteries in every shire instead of selling them and pocketing the proceeds. But that the request should have been made, and made by a man of Latimer's religious views, is indeed striking. The divergence between the letters addressed to Cromwell by the Bishop of Worcester and the Primate must enhance our respect for the courageous public spirit of the one, as it must deepen our regret for the timid inefficiency of the other.

Concurrently with his dissolution of the monasteries, Henry took up another task. He felt that the time had come to end diversities of creed among his subjects. Englishmen must be told what they were to believe, and the person to tell them was the Supreme Head of their Church. To the functions of an absolute monarch he proposed to add those of an infallible Pope. Bishops and other divines might be commissioned to frame doctrinal statements. Convocation and Parliament might be permitted to endorse them. But the authority on which they rested must be his, and his the name in which they were promulgated. In bygone years a Pope had styled him " Defender of the Faith ". He resolved to justify that title in a way that would considerably have astonished its donor. In fact, he set himself not merely to defend the Faith, but to define it. He brought to the task an acute mind, a considerable knowledge of theology, and a real respect for religion, provided always that it was not allowed to interfere with his personal morals and conduct.

The idea that all Englishmen could be

forced into an identical creed by the king's order was futile enough. Yet the time certainly was ripe for a restatement of the Church of England's position. The country seethed with religious disputes. A large number of people hardly knew what to believe. A larger number hesitated to own in public any belief at all. They waited to see, not which way the cat would jump—a figure wholly inadequate—but which way the royal lion would spring. Some desired at heart a restoration of papal control. As the faintest questioning of the royal supremacy was high treason, the minority who held this view were seldom foolish enough to air it. A far larger proportion shared the opinions of which Gardiner, Bishop of Winchester, was the leading exponent. They were insistent that the political breach with Rome and the ending of the Pope's jurisdiction should not impair the historic position of the English Church. No changes must be made which would reduce it to the level of a sect. Though papal no longer, it must remain a part of the Church Catholic.

Others, seeing and endorsing this need, yet wished the English Church to repudiate mediaeval superstitions which, though fostered by the papacy, had no primitive sanction.

Others, of whom Latimer was the principal spokesman, wished to link the old organisation of the Church with the new beliefs of Continental Protestantism. But Continental Protestantism was already divided against itself. The followers of Luther and the followers of Zwingli did not dislike the Church so bitterly as they hated one another. The Calvinists were distinct from both. The Anabaptists combined an eccentric creed with a crude socialism. All the other sects held them in contempt. For the sake of convenience, we may classify these divergent beliefs under three headings, and use terms that, strictly speaking, belong to later ages. We will describe as Romanists those who wished to restore the Pope's jurisdiction ; as Catholics those who sought to conserve, with or without minor doctrinal changes, the essential Catholicity of the English Church ; as Protestants, those who hoped to remodel the Church in accord with doctrines taught by one or other of the Continental reformers.

The king's sympathies were definitely Catholic. There were moments when he would oblige Cranmer by appointing a Protestant friend of his to a bishopric. There were times when he leaned towards the foreign policy consistently advocated by Cromwell, who wished to effect an alliance with the Protestant League of German princes. Then Henry would take what looked like a definite step in the direction of Protestantism. But those of his own subjects who so interpreted it paid bitterly for their error. Invariably it was followed by a vigorous reassertion of Catholic orthodoxy. Romanists were traitors, to be hung or beheaded. Protestants were heretics, to be burnt. On one day, July 20, 1540, six unhappy men were executed at Smithfield. Three perished on the gallows, three at the stake. Three suffered for admitting what the Pope claimed, and three for denying what the Pope believed.

Cranmer's views are more difficult to identify. It has been commonly held that they were in succession Catholic, Lutheran, and Zwinglian. This is contested by a recent writer.[1] Yet if he were never a wholehearted convert to these opinions, that his own views were modified in turn by Lutheran and Zwinglian influences seems undeniable. Apart, again, from his private beliefs, his official creed in the days of Henry VIII. was that which the king enjoined. When points

[1] By Mr. C. H. Smyth, in his careful and scholarly *Cranmer and the Reformation under Edward VI*. (Cambridge University Press, 1926.)

of doctrine were in debate, he preferred,
as he told Henry in a sentence already
quoted, to abstain from giving any decided
opinion of his own, and " to remit the judgment thereof wholly unto your majesty ".

Yet on one matter, of usage rather than
doctrine, Cranmer was admirably resolute.
He loved and honoured the English tongue.
He wrote it with a felicity of cadence that has
never been excelled. He proved that as the
language of devotion it was capable of a
sonority that Latin could not surpass and of
a flexibility it could not equal. He believed
that the growing national spirit would be both
strengthened and purified if the English
people were given an English Bible. In the
face of serious discouragement he set himself
to bring this about. The task, if in one sense
it had been facilitated, in another had been
made more difficult, and even dangerous, by
the work of William Tyndale. His diction
set up a standard which all subsequent trans-
lators, and not least the makers of the
Authorised Version, were wise enough to
follow. Yet the violently Protestant in-
troductions and notes accompanying his
New Testament not only caused it to be
publicly burnt and proscribed, but caused
some leaders of the Catholic school to view

K

any project for an English Bible with suspicion. When Cranmer proposed that a
translation should be undertaken by the
bishops, he found some of them very loth
to co-operate. It is notable, however, that
among those who consented was Gardiner.
On June 10, 1535, he wrote to Cromwell that
he was in great need of " rest and quiet for
the health of my body " owing to his recent
toil, " having finished the translation of St.
Luke and St. John, wherein I have spent a
great labour ".

But other bishops were less industrious
or more reluctant to have a share in the work,
and two years later Cranmer's hopes were
still unfulfilled. Coverdale's English Bible,
printed in 1536, was free from such contro-
versial notes as Tyndale had appended to
his New Testament, yet was on a lower level
of scholarship. But on August 4, 1537,
Cranmer sent to Cromwell " a Bible in
English, both of a new translation and a new
print. . . . I like it better than any other
translation heretofore made ". He begs
Cromwell to show this Bible to the king,

and to obtain of his grace, if you can, a licence that
the same may be sold and read of every person,
without danger of any act, proclamation or ordinance
heretofore granted to the contrary, until such time

as we the bishops shall set forth a better translation
—which I think will not be till a day after doomsday.

If Cromwell does this, Cranmer adds, God
will reward him, even though " in the mean
season you suffer some snubs and many
slanders, lies, and reproaches ".

The fear was needless. Cromwell showed
the Bible to Henry, and Henry, probably
without any close examination of it, granted
the licence for its sale and use which Cranmer
desired. Nine days later the Archbishop
expresses his gratitude with a warmth seldom
shown in his correspondence :

Whereas I understand that your lordship, at my
request, hath not only exhibited the Bible which I
sent you unto the king's majesty, but also hath
obtained of his grace that the same shall be allowed
by his authority to be bought and read within this
realm ; my lord, for this your pain taken in this
behalf I give unto you my most hearty thanks ;
assuring your lordship for the contentation of my
mind you have shewed me more pleasure herein
than if you had given me a thousand pound . . .

He writes again on August 28, to renew
" the most hearty thanks that any heart can
think ".

In point of fact, this " new translation ",
which Cranmer professed to like " better
than any other translation heretofore made ",
was not new in any part. The title-page

ascribed it to " Thomas Matthew ", who did not exist. Its actual compiler was John Rogers, a disciple of Tyndale. The New Testament version in it was entirely Tyndale's, and included some of his acrimonious notes and his Lutheran preface to the Epistle to the Romans. The Old Testament contained Tyndale's translation of such books as he had lived to complete ; the remainder were given in Coverdale's rendering. That Cranmer failed to detect the real sources of this " new translation " is incredible. But Tyndale's work had been publicly burnt by the king's command. To ask him now to permit the free circulation of the same work would have been to incur something worse than the " snubs " predicted in the Archbishop's letter. This fiction of a " new " translation by an imaginary hand served its end. It enabled the king, without evident inconsistency, to sanction a step that accorded with the religious wishes of Cranmer and the political schemes of Cromwell.

" Matthew's Bible " was revised and re-issued in 1539 as " the Great Bible ". From it comes that version of the Psalms which is still retained in our Prayer-book. Cromwell, who had secured a pecuniary interest in its sale, ordered a copy of the

Great Bible to be placed in every parish church. Its fine title-page, attributed to Holbein, depicts the distribution of this Bible by Cranmer and Cromwell, while the words "Vivat rex" issue from the mouths of the recipients. Subsequent criticisms of the Great Bible, the weightiest of which came from Gardiner, led to proposals for its revision. They were frustrated by the king. No further translation was issued within Cranmer's lifetime. An Act of 1543 attempted to restrict the privilege of Bible-reading, withdrawing it from all women except those of high birth, and from all artificers, apprentices, and others. It may be surmised that a law so difficult of enforcement had small effect. Printed copies alike of the Great Bible and its predecessors multiplied steadily. Cranmer's aim was achieved. Amid the pitiful record of his moral and administrative failures, and in welcome contrast with his habitual cowardice, we shall remember that it was he who ventured a request notably audacious, which easily might have brought about his downfall. And he it was who, by making this request, first secured for the English people the right to own and study without molestation a Bible in the English tongue.

CHAPTER VI

THE CONFLICT OF PARTIES

MEANWHILE the king, in a rapid succession of measures, had pursued the task of defining his people's creed. In 1536 appeared " Articles devised by the king's highness' majesty, to establish Christian quietness and unity among us ". The character of these ten Articles was not at variance with their title. They represented, no doubt, a genuine attempt to reconcile conflicting views. Thus they named baptism, the eucharist, and penance as sacraments necessary to salvation, but were silent concerning the other four. They enjoined the continuance of ancient ceremonies, but deprecated their superstitious use. They upheld prayer for the departed, but condemned the doctrine of purgatory. These compromises failed in their purpose. They were especially distasteful to the clergy in the north of England. Their publication, so far from " establishing quietness and unity ", was quickly followed in Lincolnshire and Yorkshire by armed revolt. Factors more potent, however, than the Articles in causing this upheaval were a new financial levy for the king's benefit and, above all, Cromwell's attack on the monasteries. The principal movement, known as " The Pilgrimage of Grace ", reached serious dimensions. It was followed by other uprisings. Henry dealt with them in characteristic fashion. He parleyed with the rebels until his reinforcement arrived. He made promises which not for a moment did he intend to keep. By such means he lured the malcontents into laying down their arms. Then he proceeded to take ferocious vengeance. Scores of reputed leaders, clerical and lay, were executed. It was not the leaders alone who suffered. No more vivid picture of the sequel can be needed than that which Henry's instructions to the Duke of Norfolk supply. " You shall in any wise cause such dreadful execution to be done upon a good number of the inhabitants of every town, village, and hamlet that have offended in this rebellion, as well by the hanging of them up in trees as by the quartering of them and the setting of their heads and quarters in every town great and small, as they may be a fearful spectacle to all other hereafter that would practise any like matter ".

The Articles having failed in their purpose, the bishops, under Cranmer's leadership, expanded them with fuller teaching into a treatise. Controversies between the followers of Gardiner and those of Latimer made the task difficult. The treatise, formally entitled " The Institution of a Christian Man ", was known popularly as " The Bishops' Book ". It was published in 1537. Henry sanctioned its circulation for a limited time, saying that he would himself examine and revise it when he could find leisure.

Another step taken by Convocation at his bidding was to reduce the number of holy days. A strange medley of reasons prompted this action. In part, it was designed to weaken the popular influence of the monasteries. Many of them had derived much fame from their possession of relics, and the veneration of relics was specially linked with holy days. On these feasts, too, sacred images were exhibited or carried in procession. Many of them were mechanical toys, which deluded few but gave childish delight to crowds of rustic sightseers. The monasteries were to go ; therefore relics and images must go with them.

Another reason alleged for the reduction of holy days was of a different kind. They were said to foster idleness, to interrupt work, and, in particular, to cause the farmers serious inconvenience at harvest time. Accordingly it was decreed that all holy days should be abrogated between July 1 and September 29. Yet we may well believe that at least the former of these dates was selected less to satisfy the farmers than to gratify the king. For if there was one saint's day in the Calendar which Henry viewed with special repugnance, that day was the feast of St. Thomas of Canterbury. And the feast of St. Thomas of Canterbury fell on July 7. That a prelate who had flouted royal authority should be revered among the saints seemed intolerable. Becket had triumphed over Henry II. Henry VIII. would triumph over Becket. First, this new veto, conveniently made operative from July 1, abolished the observance of his feast on July 7. Then in 1538 his magnificent shrine, among the most ornate and most famous in England, was destroyed, its gold and jewels handed over to the king, and the bones of the saint cast into the fire. That this outrage drew yet another excommunication from Rome did not perturb Henry. The name of St. Thomas of

Canterbury was ordered to be expunged from all service-books, and churches dedicated to him were hastily placed under the patronage of the doubting Apostle.

The contemporary Thomas of Canterbury was more concerned to obey orders than to protect the memory of his predecessor. A monk of St. Augustine's noted in his journal of 1537 : " The same year the Archbishop of Canterbury did not fast on St. Thomas' eve, but did eat flesh and did sup in his parlour with his family, which was never seen before ". On August 28 Cranmer wrote to Cromwell that " since my last coming into Kent I have found the people of my diocese very obstinately given to observe and keep with solemnity the holy days lately abrogated ". He has admonished and punished lay offenders ; he has threatened the clergy with deprivation. But he complains that his difficulties are increased by the fact that some of the forbidden feasts are still observed at court, whereby " the king's own house shall be an example unto all the realm to break his own ordinances ". But to Henry no idea could have seemed more ludicrous than that the king's majesty in his own household should be bound by laws he had imposed upon mere subjects.

Little as he intended it, the king's recent actions had encouraged the Protestants. His destruction of shrines, abrogation of saints' days, and overthrow of monasteries were altogether to their liking. Reformers at home believed that his Catholic sympathies were weakening. Reformers abroad were ill-informed enough to assert that Cromwell, whom they accounted their friend, was now the virtual ruler of England. These facts, together with the political situation on the Continent, led Cromwell to press his scheme for an alliance with the North German princes. To Cranmer they suggested an opportunity for a religious concordat with the Lutherans. The idea was misguided ; the attempt to give it effect disastrous. Three Lutheran delegates were encouraged to come to England. From the first they provoked the anger of the king and the resentment of the Catholic-minded bishops. Their tone was less that of negotiators anxious to remove difficulties than of teachers condescending to enlighten the ignorant. These " German orators ", as they were officially styled, demanded that the Church should remodel its beliefs in accordance with their views. They ruined their chance of success by denouncing as " abuses " points of doctrine to which the king attached special importance. Cranmer asked his fellow-bishops to equip him with a statement of their views. He asked in vain. " They gave me this answer ", he wrote :

that they know that the king's grace hath taken upon himself to answer the said orators in that behalf, and thereof a book is already devised by the king's majesty ; and therefore they will not meddle with the abuses, lest they should write therein contrary to that the king shall write. Wherefore they have required me to treat now of the sacraments of matrimony, orders, confirmation, and extreme unction ; wherein they know certainly that the Germans will not agree with us, except it be in matrimony only ; so that I perceive that the bishops seek only an occasion to break the concord.

In truth there was no concord to break. At an early stage the parleys broke down, and the Lutherans proposed to return home. Cranmer would have been wise to admit his failure and to speed their going. Instead, he persuaded them to remain for another month. Yet it seems unlikely that they enjoyed their visit. As the Archbishop had been unable to house them at Lambeth, a lodging had been found for them by Cromwell, of which Cranmer complains on their behalf that " besides the multitude of rats daily and nightly running in their chambers, which is no small disquietness, the kitchen standeth directly against their parlour where they daily dine and sup, and by reason thereof the house savoureth so ill that it offendeth all men that come into it ".

The results of Cranmer's unlucky scheme did not end with the departure of the Lutheran delegates. Consequences were yet to follow, of a kind little desired or expected by the Archbishop. The king determined that there should be no further misunderstandings of his attitude. Many of his subjects, including Cranmer, seemed to imagine that he was veering towards Protestantism. He would take steps to undeceive them. In 1539 an Act was to be passed to ratify the destruction of the last monasteries. No Lutherans in consequence should hail him as a convert to their detestable creed. He commanded Parliament to pass a statute grimly described by himself as " An Act abolishing diversity in opinions ", and by the Protestants as " the whip with six strings ". This was the Statute of Six Articles. It reaffirmed the three points attacked by the Lutherans and three others : (i.) transubstantiation ; (ii.) communion in one kind ; (iii.) clerical celibacy ; (iv.) religious vows ; (v.) private masses ; (vi.) auricular confession. The debates on these matters in the House of

Peers showed that there was little chance of " abolishing diversity in opinion " among lay folk when the Archbishop of Canterbury and five bishops spoke for the reformers, the Archbishop of York and four bishops for the conservatives. At length Henry, as the preamble of the Act narrated,

most graciously vouchsafed in his own princely person to descend and come into his said high Court of Parliament, and there like a prince of most high prudence and no less learning opened and declared many things of great knowledge touching the said articles. . . .

The king's appearance on the scene was decisive. Writing ten years later, when Henry was dead and the Act repealed, Cranmer described the Six Articles as " so enforced by the evil counsel of certain papists, against the truth and common judgment of divines and lawyers, that if the king's majesty himself had not come personally into the Parliament house, these laws had never passed ".

The sting of the measure lay not in its doctrinal statements, but in the enacting and penal clauses which followed them. Henceforth all who questioned the mediaeval dogma of transubstantiation were to be burnt as heretics, and not they only, but all " their aiders, comforters, counsellors, consenters, and abettors therein ". Those who expressed opinions contrary to any of the other five Articles were to be adjudged felons, and " to suffer pains of death as in cases of felony ". In effect this was a " Verbal Heresy " Act, the counterpart of the Verbal Treasons Act passed six years earlier. It established a reign of terror. Spies were ubiquitous, for to play the informer's part was a sure road to promotion. Any casual remark which malice could twist into a doubt of transubstantiation brought its speaker within measurable distance of the stake.

The bishops of Protestant sympathies found themselves in a most uncomfortable position. Latimer resigned his see of Worcester, and Shaxton his of Salisbury. Cranmer, we may suppose, was less perturbed by the enforcement of transubstantiation than by the disallowing of clerical marriage. His sacramental views were still somewhat nebulous. Mistress Cranmer was a definite fact. Her presence rendered the Primate liable to indictment as a felon, and therefore he deported her to Germany. For this he cannot be blamed, but his prosecution of clergy for offences akin to his own is difficult to justify. The Statute of Six Articles was passed in the summer of 1539. In August of that year Cranmer wrote to Cromwell, enclosing his examination of a priest and a woman " very suspiciously taken ", and asking how the king would have him secure " the due correction and punishment of all such offenders according to the Act in this behalf ". Cranmer's personal record and his heartfelt dislike of the Act combine to make this letter peculiarly odious. Its motive is clear. As he might have offended the king by opposing this measure in debate, he would conciliate the king by his active support of the measure now that it had become law.

The year 1539 saw Henry's autocracy carried to its extreme height. By the Statute of Six Articles he established his claim to define the religious beliefs permissible for his people. Yet its passage through Parliament had not been secured without difficulty. Therefore in the same session he followed it with another Act, abandoning his last pretence of constitutional procedure, and making him independent of Parliamentary support. It decreed that henceforth all royal proclamations should " be obeyed, observed, and kept as though they were made by Act of Parliament ". Thus the last check to his despotism was removed. For the remainder of his reign he enjoyed an absolutism without parallel in the history of England. Being resolved to keep all power, ecclesiastical and civil, in his own hands, he had no further need of minister or vicar-general. Cromwell had served his turn. His industry, as vigorous and able as it was unscrupulous, had been of special service to Henry in two matters ; the spoiling of the monasteries and the packing of the House of Commons. The former task was now complete. The latter was no longer needed. Moreover, Cromwell was beginning to acquire more influence than Henry wished any subject to possess. Arrogance fatal to a Wolsey certainly would not be permitted to a Cromwell.

As matters shaped themselves, Cromwell precipitated his own downfall. He did his master a wrong which, beyond any other, was unlikely to be forgiven. Jane Seymour had died shortly after giving birth to her son Edward. Henry was considering how he might obtain at the same time another wife and some political advantage. Projects for a marriage with a French princess were formed, but came to nothing. Then Cromwell, still bent on his Protestant foreign policy, imprudently brought about the betrothal of Henry VIII. and the sister of the

L

powerful Duke of Cleves. Cranmer was instructed to welcome the bride at Canterbury as she journeyed to London, and to make her a present of money. Anne of Cleves, as Henry must have known, was thirty-four years of age. Yet, if no longer young, she was reported to be attractive and clever. To his dismay, she proved to be plain and stupid. Not for any political advantage would the connoisseur in wives tolerate such a union as this, or pardon the man who had lured him into it. On April 17, 1540, Cromwell had been advanced to the Earldom of Essex. On June 10 he was arrested in the king's council-chamber. A hasty bill of attainder condemned him to death. On July 9 Cranmer and both Houses of Convocation went through the now familiar routine of declaring yet another of Henry's marriages to be null and void. On July 28 Cromwell was beheaded at Tyburn. On August 8 Henry married Katharine Howard, a lady of considerable beauty and no character. As for Anne of Cleves, with the best grace imaginable she withdrew her claim to be accounted Henry's wife, thanked him for his kindness, accepted two manors and an annuity of £4000, and so retired, doubtless praising Heaven that she was well quit of the business.

Cromwell's fall was a staggering blow to Cranmer. He had obeyed the vicar-general without question and trusted him without reserve. Enough for him that Cromwell seemed the king's faithful minister. He was unperturbed by the knowledge that the faithful minister, in the process of stealing colossal sums for his master, had acquired by ways less open but equally nefarious a large fortune for himself. " I loved him as my friend ", wrote the archbishop to the king, " for so I took him to be ; but I chiefly loved him for the love which I thought I saw him bear ever towards your grace ." A modern historian has cited this letter as proof of Cranmer's " courage ", asserting that he alone " interceded " for Cromwell. It is probably true that there was scarcely another man in England to whom Cromwell's fate was not a cause of joy. Yet the " intercession " was indeed of a dubious sort, for Cranmer adds that " I am very glad that his treason is discovered in time ", and prays God " to send such a counsellor in his place whom your grace may trust ". That is hardly a moving plea for his friend's life. But it must be admitted that Cranmer was in no position to risk such a plea. The general belief was that Cromwell's fate would be his own. As a chronicler of the period observed, " there should have been laid thousands of pounds to hundreds in London that he should have been set up in the Tower beside his friend the Lord Cromwell ".

But the wagers were lost, and, little as he realised it, Cranmer was to gain in every way by Cromwell's disappearance. For five years his primacy had been little else than nominal. On every matter of importance he had begged Cromwell's advice or taken his orders. He did not figure at court or in the king's council. To Cromwell he wrote when he would ask a favour of the king or desired to learn his majesty's pleasure. He was seldom in London, and Lambeth was so little used that without special preparation it could not accommodate three visitors. Cranmer passed most of these years, as his letters show, in one or other of his rural manors, a mere spectator of events, while Cromwell issued injunctions to the clergy. The consequences would have been less disastrous had Cromwell been more upright or Cranmer less impressionable. Any reader who examines closely the very numerous letters that passed from Cranmer to Cromwell will notice their gradual change of tone. Courtly patronage merges into equality, and equality into servility. Far worse is the moral decline. The plastic temperament begins to reproduce the unlovely characteristics of the stronger personality. Cromwell was by nature a ruthless persecutor. Cranmer was by nature amiable and kindly. Yet Cranmer too begins to delight in arresting and examining miserable delinquents before passing them on to Cromwell. " If they once look you in the face ", he writes with sniggering malice, " they should have no power to conceal anything from you ". Again, he chides Cromwell for his delay in punishing a friar who has " preached against the king's great cause " :

> I delivered unto you about Easter last past, or else afore, a certain billet concerning such matters as the same friar Oliver preached in the last Lent, which bill if ye had remembered, I doubt not that ye would have provided for the same friar before this time. . . .

—the things " provided " by Cromwell for such offenders being always prison, sometimes torture, and not seldom the gallows.

Only while under Cromwell's influence did the Archbishop attempt this repulsive type of humour, so strangely at variance with his worthier self. Cromwell had been his evil genius. Indeed, all England sighed with relief when he fell. The royal tyranny remained, yet it was no longer a corrupt tyranny. The bluff despotism of the irascible king was at least better than the espionage and chill cruelty of his rapacious vicar-general.

With the lapse of this office, the primacy regained something of its due importance. A strong archbishop Cranmer could never be, yet henceforth his word carried some weight, he was in direct touch with the king, and he became the leader, not indeed of the English Church, but at least of a party within it. His opposition to the Six Articles had identified him publicly with the reformers, and his private sympathies tended increasingly towards their less extreme beliefs. On the other side the Romanists had joined forces with the Catholics, and they were led most efficiently by Gardiner. Through the remaining years of Henry's reign there was a keen struggle between the Catholics and Protestants to dominate the Church, and an equally sharp personal conflict between Cranmer and Gardiner to influence the king. Fortune seemed to favour each party in turn. The issue was undecided up to the day when Henry's death gave a new shape to public affairs. In 1538, for example, the Protestants were sanguine of success. By 1541 the Six

Articles, the fate of Cromwell, and the king's marriage with a Howard had shown the Catholic cause to be uppermost. The king himself attended devoutly at Catholic ceremonies, presided in person at the trial of a heretic, and hanged a citizen of London for the crime of eating flesh on a Friday. But in 1541 the new queen was convicted of immorality, and like Anne Boleyn, if with less injustice, perished on the scaffold. In 1543 Henry took for his sixth and last wife a lady of Protestant sympathies. In 1545 Cranmer was so hopeful of the king's conversion to Protestant views that he drafted a royal order to forbid ancient ceremonies in which the king himself but a few years earlier had taken part. But at the last moment Gardiner intervened, and managed to convince Henry that signature would be impolitic.

Thus, year by year, the struggle continued. It was conducted not by public debate but by private intrigue. The king's council was the battle-field. Each side aimed far less at refuting rival doctrines than at destroying rival leaders. Each side plotted to arouse the king's easily-stirred anger against the chiefs of the other. Protestants felt that ancient superstitions would best be overcome by the imprisonment of Gardiner. Catholics thought that, with Cranmer safely in the Tower, the triumph of their views would be assured. Even the queen's downfall was the object of one of these conspiracies. Those who planned it were, after all, not without precedents to encourage them. But the same precedents served to put Katharine Parr on her guard. A widow when she married Henry, she was not inexpert in the management of a quick-tempered husband. With strict virtue and a religious mind she united tact and common sense. She gave her enemies no handle for adding her name to those of Katharine of Aragon, Anne Boleyn, Anne of Cleves, and Katharine Howard in the list of the king's discarded wives.

Cranmer also escaped all the plots of his enemies, owing his rescue in each instance less to his own wisdom than to the unabated favour shown him by Henry. When a member named Gostwick attacked him in Parliament, Henry sent a message that he would " make him a poor Gostwick " if such language were repeated. When some prebendaries of Cranmer's own cathedral demanded a commission to inquire into the Archbishop's alleged heresies, the king with sardonic humour granted the commission but placed the Archbishop himself at the head of it. A more threatening intrigue was hatched in the king's council ; an intrigue picturesquely treated in Fletcher and Shakespeare's play of *Henry VIII*. The dramatists have utilised the narrative of Ralph Morice, Cranmer's faithful secretary, who was himself a witness of the scenes he describes. Cranmer's enemies on the council had prevailed so far as to secure an order for his committal to the Tower. At eleven o'clock on the night before the order was to be executed the king hastily sent for Cranmer. He was in bed, but rose and accompanied the messenger from Lambeth to Whitehall. The king told him what had happened. The guileless Archbishop thanked Henry, but said he would be quite content to sojourn for a while in the Tower while the charges brought against him were investigated. " O Lord God ! " shouted the king : " what fond simplicity have you to permit yourself to be imprisoned, that every enemy of yours may take advantage against you ! Do you not know that when they have you once in prison three or four false knaves will soon be procured to witness against you and condemn you ? " Therewith he gave Cranmer his ring, which he was to produce if needful to the council, as proof that the king had taken the matter into his own hands.

After a short night—for the council met at eight in the morning—Cranmer presented himself at the doors of the council-chamber. They were closed against him. He was ordered to wait outside with the lackeys. His indignant secretary took counsel with Dr. Butts, his majesty's physician. Dr. Butts hurried away to the king, reporting that " my lord of Canterbury is become a lackey or a serving-man ; for to my knowledge he hath stood among them this hour almost at the council-chamber door ". " Have they used my lord so ? " said the king grimly. " It is well enough. I shall talk with them by and by." Meanwhile Cranmer had been admitted to the chamber and told that he was to be taken to the Tower forthwith. To the consternation of his enemies he produced the royal ring. The council had to come before the king and to hear some extremely pungent comments on their behaviour. The Duke of Norfolk replied that they had only proposed to imprison Cranmer in order that " he might after his trial be set at liberty to his greater glory " ; hardly a convincing plea. Henry bade them understand that " I count my lord of Canterbury as faithful a man towards me as ever was prelate in this realm, and one to whom I am many ways beholden ". " And so ", Morice concludes his narrative, " the king departed, and the lords shook hands every man with the archbishop ; against whom never more after durst any man spurn during King Henry's life."

Indeed Henry was too wise to lose the assistance of this most useful and pliable of servants. Cranmer might have his private heresies, but he could be trusted not to urge them against the king's wishes. His belief in the king's infallibility was unshaken. The Primate who had witnessed uncomplainingly the spoliation of the monasteries in 1536 would make no trouble when, in 1546, the king proceeded to rob the chantries. Moreover, Cranmer was wholly free from the self-seeking ambition which had brought about the fall of Wolsey and of Cromwell. " *Ego et rex meus* " was not a sentence which could come from his pen.

Of the king's religious sympathies during the last years of his reign it is difficult to speak with confidence. Cranmer declared afterwards that Henry died when he was on the verge of making drastic changes in the Protestant direction. That Cranmer honestly believed this is clear. That the king spoke honestly when he induced this belief seems more dubious. Yet there are indications that he was moving towards the reformers' views on certain points. On one, however, he was consistently inflexible. He would listen to no plea for the relaxation of clerical celibacy. His motive was utilitarian rather than doctrinal. Were the clergy permitted to marry, he said, they and their progeny would so increase as to become " a danger to princes ".

Neither the conflict of parties within the Church nor the growth of eccentric heresies outside it caused the king to abandon his ideal. He desired still an official creed, drafted in consultation with divines of various opinions, promulgated by himself, and by his sole authority made binding upon every man and woman in England. The Articles of 1535 and the Bishops' Book of the following year had been contrived for this purpose and had failed. In 1540 a commission of bishops was appointed to revise and expand the Bishops' Book. Henry himself annotated his copy in great detail and sent it to Cranmer. Cranmer in turn corrected the king's corrections. In performing this task he laid aside all his usual timidity. So far from being servile, he was barely civil. On every other matter he felt bound to take the king's word for law. But conscience did not constrain him to believe that Henry's English was better than his own, or that he must tolerate inept phrasing because it came from a royal pen. He dealt with the king's emendations as a schoolmaster would deal with a slovenly exercise. " This obscureth the sentence, and is superfluous." " This also obscureth the sense." " The praeter tense may not conveniently be joined with the present tense." " It is small difference between ' cure ' and ' charge ', but that the one is plain English and the other deducted from the Latin." " I can perceive no good cause why these words should be put in here ; they come in very strangely." Such was the fashion in which the Archbishop criticised Henry's suggestions. A careful collation of the Bishops' Book with the king's notes, Cranmer's remarks on those notes, and the new book ultimately issued, will show that at most points of difference Cranmer's view prevailed against the king's. A striking exception, however, is to be found in the sixth petition of the Lord's Prayer. " Let us not be led into temptation " was the rendering desired by the king. In this, consciously or not, he was following a very early gloss mentioned with approval by St. Augustine of Hippo : " *ne nos patiaris induci in tentationem* ". Cranmer demurred, remarking : " Christ taught us thus to pray, ' Lead us not into temptation,' and we should not alter any word in the Scripture ". But the king insisted on his version, and " let us not be led into temptation " was the form adopted. It continued to be the authorised wording until 1549, when the Book of Common Prayer was issued, and Cranmer had his way.

The making of the official treatise emphasised the divisions among the episcopate. Cranmer found some of his fellow-bishops far less tractable than the king. More than once it seemed that the project must be abandoned. But Henry was insistent, Cranmer yielded to pressure, and at length the work appeared. It was " Imprinted at London in Fleet Street by Thomas Barthelet, printer to the king's highness, the 29th day of May, in the year of our Lord 1543 ". Its full title ran : " A Necessary Erudition for any Christian man, set forth by the king's majesty of England ". Ordinarily it was described as " the King's Book ". It is a work of high literary worth and of great historic value. Though some of its doctrinal statements are not such as Cranmer would have wished, it is to him that we may attribute its sonorous yet most lucid style. The introductory chapter on " Faith " is certainly his, for it follows closely a printed homily by him on the same theme. Often, too, the formal expositions ascend at their close to a level which none but a master of English could have reached. We may take for example a few sentences near the end of the chapters on the Apostles' Creed. They speak of " the life everlasting ":

> Yea, there is no joy or comfort that can be wished for but it is there most plentifully. There is true glory, where praise shall be without error or flattery. There is true honour, which shall be given to none except he be worthy. There is true peace, where no man shall be molested or grieved, neither by himself nor by others. There is true and pleasant fellowship, where is the company of blessed angels, and the elect and chosen saints of God. There is true and perfect love, which never shall fail. For all the heavenly company is linked and fastened together by the bond of perfect charity ; whereby also they be united and knit to Almighty God everlastingly.

The historical value of the King's Book lies in its demarcation of the limits to which the Reformation was carried under Henry VIII. The papal claims are vigorously attacked. The doctrine of indulgences and purgatory is repudiated. On the other hand, transubstantiation, communion in one kind, and clerical celibacy are upheld.

Cranmer was also instructed by the king to prepare a Litany in English. This appeared in 1545. With the omission of a few clauses, including a petition for deliverance from the " detestable enormities " of the Pope, it stands to-day in our Prayer-book precisely as Cranmer wrote it, one of the noblest fruits of his great liturgical genius.

But the devotions of the litany and the instructions of the King's Book were alike powerless to end religious discord. There was no town or village in England unperturbed by its malign influence. On the Christmas Eve of 1545 the king spoke mournfully to Parliament of this evil. He deplored the sectarian spirit. He deprecated the readiness of each party to assail as papists or as heretics those who differed from it. He bade all keep in mind the apostolic praise of charity. It was an admirable speech. But its effect might have been greater had Henry shown the least sign of putting his doctrine into practice. In the new year prosecutions of heretics were frequent. In July the Statute of Six Articles was revived. Anne Askew, a Lincolnshire lady, and three men were burnt at the stake for denying transubstantiation. With equal zeal Henry continued to attack all whom he deemed his political enemies. He suspected the Howards of plotting a change in the succession. The Duke of Norfolk and his son were condemned. On January 19, 1547, Surrey was executed. Norfolk was to die on January 28. But when that morning broke, the king himself lay dead.

So passed the strongest man that ever held and misused the powers of the English crown ; without peer as a ruffianly tyrant, yet matched only by his daughter Elizabeth as a judge of character. We need not pause to estimate afresh that tremendous personality. Many rejoiced heartily at his death. Some, and those the most clear-sighted, wondered if the uncertain future might not hold yet worse trials for England. But one man lamented with utter sorrow ; a sorrow so intense that it would go unhealed to his own dying day. The guileless heart of one man came near to breaking when Henry VIII. died. And that man was Thomas Cranmer.

M

CHAPTER VII

CRANMER AND PROTESTANTISM

THE death of Henry VIII. ended his system of government. This was, indeed, inevitable. A system based upon the personal autocracy of the king could not continue when the king was a boy of nine. Foreseeing this, Henry had attempted to ensure a renewal of royal despotism for Edward on his coming of age. Through the intervening years a council of regency should conduct the necessary business of government. But its powers were to be limited. The statute sanctioning its creation stipulated also that Edward on reaching his majority should have the right to annul any action taken by the council. Such was the scheme which Henry devised. Such was not the scheme carried into effect. With the fierce old king in his grave and his terrifying presence no longer among them, the council set aside his wishes. They appointed a Protector, with powers beyond any that

Henry would have permitted to a subject. The Act enabling Edward to repeal their ordinances was itself repealed. Not content with political ascendancy, they sought to exercise the ecclesiastical authority which Henry had claimed as Head of the Church. Their methods of rule quickly made them odious. If the tyranny of Henry had been hard to bear, at least it had been the tyranny of an Englishman and a king. It was replaced by the tyranny of greedy adventurers, employing foreign troops to coerce Englishmen and foreign divines to instruct them.

The reign of Edward VI. lasted but six-and-a-half years. The evil it wrought to the realm was out of all proportion to its length. It was marked by mismanagement of public affairs at home and abroad. To the Church it brought pillage of goods, anarchy of government, and attacks upon fundamental doctrines. In such a crisis the powers of the strongest archbishop would have been taxed to the uttermost. In such an age the unhappy weakness of Cranmer became increasingly evident and increasingly disastrous. Through five of the seven years since his consecration he had leaned upon Cromwell. For another seven he had been able to refer each question of doctrine or practice directly to the king. Now he had either to think and act for himself, or to take his orders from men whom, with ample cause, he despised. He had either to forget his belief in royal infallibility or to suppose the divine wisdom of a king to be temporarily vested in a syndicate of rascals. As a matter of fact he attempted, with dismal results, to combine both views. He would not obey the Protector and council without question, as he had obeyed Henry. Up to a point, he resisted demands upon him which he knew to be wrong. But at that point his custom was to yield, persuading himself that it must be right to render unwillingly to the king's representatives that deference which he had rendered willingly to the king.

In matters of religious belief, however, he had more freedom after Henry's death. Not even Cranmer could quite accept a Somerset or a Northumberland as the authorised exponent of Christian truth. For some years his private beliefs on the crucial matter of Eucharistic doctrine had been fluctuating and confused. But of his public standpoint there could be no doubt. Henry kept an unaltered faith in transubstantiation, and by the Statute of Six Articles had ordered his people to accept this dogma without question. Cranmer's rule of life compelled him to regard the king's decision as final. Until Henry's death he neither wrote nor spoke a word against transubstantiation. That his private judgment doubted, if it had not definitely rejected, the belief by 1543 is clear. Yet in 1543 he had a chief share in issuing the *Necessary Erudition*, which affirmed the dogma in its most unequivocal form. Only when Henry was dead did the Archbishop of Canterbury think himself free to state in public the doctrinal views which he had long held in private.

Even then his avowed creed was not, in any complete sense, his own. But now at least it was derived from an honest theologian, instead of from an immoral king. Nicholas Ridley had been Master of Pembroke College, Cambridge. Afterwards he spent three years abroad, and there found himself in sympathy with some of the Continental reformers. On his return he became one of the Archbishop's chaplains. His was a somewhat narrow yet clear and vigorous intellect. If he refused to believe anything he did not know, at least he knew what he believed. Soon he became the authority to whom Cranmer, ever unable to stand alone, referred his doctrinal perplexities, and Ridley's sacramental beliefs became those of Cranmer. In his examination after his arrest the Archbishop said frankly that he had held mistaken sacramental views until " Dr. Ridley did confer with me, and by sundry persuasions and authorities of doctors drew me quite from my opinion ".

The Eucharistic controversies of the sixteenth century form a subject far too large and intricate for detailed consideration in these pages. Here we are concerned with them merely so far as they had a direct bearing upon Cranmer's career. That bearing, however, may be understood more readily if we summarise, though briefly and inadequately, a few of the more important beliefs held by various schools of thought in his time.

(a) The early Church had taught the Real and Spiritual presence of the Body and Blood of Christ in the consecrated elements without attempting to define the mode and nature of that Presence. (b) The doctrine of transubstantiation, based upon the involved philosophy of the Middle Ages, taught that the elements at consecration underwent a substantial change, so that the Body and Blood took the place of the bread and wine. (c) At the opposite pole from this view was that of Zwingli and his school. It reduced the Sacrament to the level of a mere commemorative rite, denying any special Presence of Christ and any special grace bestowed upon the receiver. (*d*) Calvin, followed with slight differences by Bucer and others, admitted the truth of a Real Presence, but held that it was subjective, not objective—in other words, that it was a Presence communicated to the soul of the worthy receiver, but not inherent in the Sacrament itself. The words of consecration left the elements precisely what they were : the faith of the communicant enabled him to receive the Body and Blood of Christ.

This, known as the " receptionist " theory, was accepted by Ridley, and taught by him to Cranmer. Through the rest of his life Cranmer seems to have fluctuated between the receptionist and the Zwinglian beliefs. A recent historian has argued that he " never became a Zwinglian ". That, in a sense, is true. His beliefs were so indeterminate that at no time could he be described as belonging definitely to one school. Yet, if he never became a Zwinglian, unquestionably from time to time he shared Zwinglian views. A speech which he delivered in December 1548 was greeted triumphantly by the

Zwinglians as proof of his conversion. Passages in his later writings, again, seem Zwinglian in their tone ; as, for example, when he affirms of our Lord that " no more truly is He corporally or really present in the due ministration of the Lord's Supper than He is in the due ministration of baptism ". In fact, Cranmer's sacramental opinions were varying and inconsistent. Unable to arrive at clear convictions for himself, he was easily swayed by any dogmatic friend in whose company he chanced to be.

When Edward came to the throne there had been no official change in the formularies of the English Church. Under Henry the Reformation had been limited to a political movement which repudiated the papal juris-diction and a social movement which over-threw the monasteries. At his death the authorised beliefs and ceremonial of the English Church were virtually what they had been at his accession. Yet the growth of the new learning made it certain that modifications of doctrine must follow the political and social changes. That they were to come in this sequence was most fortunate. Neither poli-tical nor social change had touched the essential character of the English Church. Its bishops, clergy, convocation and sacraments had continued in an unbroken line. When the time came to purify its doctrine from mediaeval errors, the process could be carried out by the Church itself, without loss of Catholicity and without reference to the Pope. On the Continent, where religious changes preceded the political breach with Rome, this was impossible. Thus the course of events in the sixteenth century led on the Continent to the formation of new religious bodies, in England to the re-formation of the historic Church. Continental Protestantism could not be taken over as the religion of England. It contained elements of truth. But it contained also doctrines subversive of the Church's fundamental position. Their adoption would have reduced the English Church to the level of a sect. To utilise the new learning for the purifying and enrichment of its teaching, yet to preserve its essential character as a part of the Catholic Church of Christ, was the ideal kept in view by the more moderate Reformers.

But the men into whose hands fell the government of the realm in 1547 were not moderate. For three days Henry's death was concealed from the nation. Then the names of the council of regency were disclosed. They caused general surprise. It had been supposed that Henry would include the leaders of various parties, while securing a preponderance for men of his own views. Yet almost all the sixteen appointed were known to be on the Protestant side. If there was a name which everyone expected to figure on the list, it was that of Stephen Gardiner. He had seemed to stand high in the king's favour. He was unquestionably the leader of the anti-papal Catholics. The omission of his name, viewed in conjunction with the strange delay in announcing Henry's death, stirred some ugly suspicions. Was the will produced the will as Henry had made it? It had been through the hands of Paget, the king's secretary, and certainly Paget was a man who would not scruple to tamper with a document. Yet it is most improbable that he did so in this instance, for the absence of Gardiner from the list, strange as it seemed at the moment, is intelligible enough. We can attribute it confidently to the influence of Cranmer. He had been the king's close friend through Henry's last years, and had ministered to him on his deathbed. Between Cranmer and Gardiner the antagonism was as bitter as it was notorious. We need not think that Cranmer urged the exclusion of his foe from the council of regency. His attitude would make a direct request super-fluous. Henry desired to choose a body of men who would work well together in the task of government through the difficult years of his son's minority. To give both Cranmer and Gardiner seats at the council table would have been to make the chances of harmonious co-operation small indeed.

The initial act of the council was to nominate Lord Hertford, the new king's uncle, as Protector. He was given the title of Duke of Somerset. Other honours were distributed freely by the council among them-selves, in the pretence that this was a fulfil-ment of the late king's intentions. Then the council required the bishops to take out new licences for the discharge of their functions. This order may have been issued at Cranmer's suggestion. Certainly it had his approval. It served to emphasise his view that all spiritual authority was derived from the crown, and that the officers of the Church were the servants of the state. Gardiner and some other bishops protested vainly. Somerset himself was a narrow, ill-informed, but sincere Protestant. To most of his associates Protestantism stood as the agency which had confiscated Church posses-sions for the late king, and as the agency which, they trusted, soon would confiscate further Church possessions for the new king's councillors. Protestantism, therefore, had their ready support.

At Edward's accession no new formulary of belief had been issued since the *Necessary Erudition* of 1543. This, accordingly, promulgated as " the King's Book ", and ratified by Convocation, remained the official exposition of Church doctrine. Its point of view was, as we have seen, both definitely Catholic and definitely anti-papal. But change clearly was imminent. The attitude of Protector and council showed that it must come. The attitude of Cranmer showed that the Primate would not oppose its coming. Significantly enough, the conducting of Henry's obsequies, with the full ceremonial of ancient usage, was left to Gardiner. But it was Cranmer who preached at Edward's coronation. He likened the hapless child to Josiah, ardent reformer and destroyer of images.

The comparison was ominous. Four months later the first steps were taken towards its literal fulfilment. In July 1547 the council issued a set of " injunctions " to the clergy, on the lines of those set forth by Cromwell in 1538. They commanded the removal of all images, pictures, and monuments that were

liable to "abuse" through pilgrimages or
other superstitious usage. A visitation in the
king's name was to follow, lest in any church
the injunctions should have been defied. In
fact they were defied at this stage, both widely
and with impunity. An incumbent could
plead that the images in his church had not
been "abused", and accordingly were not
condemned by the injunctions. Therefore
the distinction was cancelled by a fresh set of
injunctions, issued in the following February.
They ordered the removal of all images,
whether abused or not. When removed,
however, they were not always destroyed.
They, with many of the exquisitely illumin-
ated service-books of former generations,
were still treasured in private hands. To
complete their work, the fanatical iconoclasts
provided by an Act of 1550 fines or imprisonment for all who "hereafter shall have in
their custody any the books or writings aforesaid, or any images of stone, timber, alabaster,
or earth, graven, carved or painted, which
heretofore have been taken out of any church
or chapel".

The loss thus inflicted on sacred art is not
easy to compute. Priceless missals and other
service-books were burnt as refuse. Windows
were smashed, shrines broken up, tombs

defaced, frescoes obliterated with whitewash.
A wealth of ornament had glorified our
ancient churches. The whole buildings
gleamed with gold and colour. Above the
frescoed walls the scheme was continued by
the radiant stained glass of the clerestory.
Many a great perpendicular church seems
to-day, despite its nobility of proportion, chill
and forbidding. But its wide wall-spaces
were not meant to be bare or its windows
glazed with plain glass. Our judgment would
be changed could we have seen it in its
pristine glory, bright-hued from floor to roof.
Much of the damage to our parish churches
popularly attributed to Oliver Cromwell was
in fact perpetrated a century earlier by the
commissioners of Edward VI. Amid the
general havoc made by the Act of 1550, we
may note that it exempted from destruction
"the images of any king, prince, nobleman, or
other dead person, that hath not been
commonly reputed and taken for a saint".
The result is poignantly illustrated in the
Cathedral church of Worcester. The images
of Oswald, its founder, and Wulfstan, its
great bishop and benefactor, were destroyed,
for the names of Oswald and Wulfstan had
places in the Calendar of Saints. Between
their shrines, in the centre of the choir, were

the tomb and figure of King John. Not the most eager iconoclast could maintain that King John had ever been " reputed and taken for a saint ". Therefore his image was spared, and retains still its incongruous and conspicuous position.

On the day when the Injunctions of 1547 were published there appeared also a Book of Homilies for use by the clergy. Cranmer had planned such a book five years earlier, and at that time had received the promise of Gardiner's assistance in writing it. But Henry did not look favourably on the project, and it lapsed. When Cranmer revived his idea in 1547, Gardiner emphatically refused to co-operate. He did so for two reasons. First, he held that the royal supremacy was vested in the person of the king and could not be delegated to the council. Changes in religion, he said, should be deferred until the king had come of age. Secondly, he reminded Cranmer that his earlier promise had been given before the publication of *The King's Book*. This supplied the need of an authoritative exposition of doctrine and was still in force. It had been promulgated by the crown and approved by Parliament and Convocation. Therefore the issue of a book of homilies to modify or supersede it was not

merely unnecessary but illegal. The Archbishop's reply ignored the change in his own
religious beliefs and attacked *The King's Book*.
He alleged that Henry had been " seduced "
into its adoption. This was a remarkable
statement to come from the Primate, who himself had taken a chief share in writing and
publishing the work, and it enabled Gardiner
to make an effective retort :

After your Grace hath four years continually
lived in agreement of that doctrine under our late
sovereign lord, now so suddenly after his death to
write to me that his highness was seduced, it is,
I assure you, a very strange speech. As often as
your Grace shall say he was seduced you shall more
touch yourself than him, in that ye told him not so
in his life.

The Archbishop of Canterbury and the
Bishop of Winchester continued to exchange
such letters. Gardiner also addressed his
protests to Somerset. He denounced the
injunctions and visitation. He denounced
the *Paraphrase* of Erasmus which, with its
Protestant notes, was to be placed in every
church.   He denounced the teaching of
Cranmer's homilies.   He denounced the
action of the council in making religious
changes during the king's minority. So
candid were his words and so considerable
his influence that the council was afraid to

leave him at large. Various short terms of confinement failed to silence him, and at length he was sent to the Tower for the remainder of the reign. His fate was soon to be shared by Bonner, Bishop of London, whose views were more extreme. From the Tower Gardiner continued to attack Cranmer's theology, and Cranmer replied at vast length. The letters grew to tracts ; the tracts to treatises. When the time came for Cranmer to die, Gardiner was already dead. Yet he avowed that his chief regret was to leave incomplete his last voluminous reply to Gardiner's last voluminous attack. Personal animus had a part in this warfare. Gardiner attributed his imprisonment to Cranmer's enmity. Time was to bring him his chance of revenge.

Through ten months Protector and council had ruled by proclamations issued on their own authority, in the manner of the late king, without recourse to Parliament. But in November 1547 both Convocation and Parliament met. Convocation petitioned for an Act to legalise clerical marriage. When this was granted in the following session, Cranmer's wife was able, after an absence of seven years, to rejoin her husband. Parliament passed a number of important measures. The most

N

laudable repealed the Statute of Six Articles and the Treason Acts of Henry, declaring that

as in tempest or winter one course and garment is convenient, in calm or warm weather a more liberal race or lighter garment both may and ought to be followed, so we have seen divers strait and sore laws made in one Parliament, the time so requiring, in a more calm and quiet reign of another prince by like authority and Parliament repealed and taken away.

Less praiseworthy were the other enactments of this session. Bishops were no longer to be elected by Dean and Chapter but nominated by letters patent from the crown. It might be urged that the right of election was worthless when the crown's nominee was forced on the electors, and that the new procedure was in effect no more than the old stripped of pretence. Yet the difference made by the Act of 1547 was real and deplorable. With the *congé d'élire* abolished, the bishops were appointed solely by letters patent. Therefore they became liable to dismissal whenever the king should think fit, for letters patent might be withdrawn at any time. More definitely than any previous legislation this Act made the bishops mere state officials. The crown placed them in office, and the crown could eject them at will.

Yet another Act of this session continued that destruction of chantries and chapels which Henry VIII. had begun. More than two thousand were now to be swept away. In theory, their revenues were to be used for the promotion of education and the relief of the poor. In practice, the greater part were transferred to the pockets of the council.

The " calm and quiet reign " which the Treasons Act of 1547 had extolled was not easily to be recognised in the events of this and the succeeding years. Indeed the Act itself, desirable as was its repeal of brutal penalties, contributed to the general disorder of the time. Religious differences had seldom been aired in public, while even to whisper a doubt of transubstantiation was a capital offence. Now the penal laws had disappeared. The commanding and terrifying influence of Henry was gone. Men were free to debate religion as they chose, and chose often to use that liberty unchecked by reverence. Every type of doctrine, from that which would seem orthodox at Rome to that which would be thought extreme at Geneva, was preached with equal confidence from the pulpits of the English Church. Laymen whose know-ledge was not proportionate to their zeal argued at large over the most abstruse points

of theology. In one parish the old ceremonial would be maintained and the old
scheme of fasts and festivals punctiliously
observed. In the next parish a reforming
incumbent would denounce ceremonial and
saints' days alike as inventions of Satan.
The council's emissaries roamed through the
land destroying " images ", while folk whose
ancestors had been commemorated by altar-
tomb or stained window looked on in powerless resentment. The Protector himself resolved to pull down Westminster Abbey, in
order to use its stones for the building of his
own palace. The Dean and Chapter had to
buy him off with a bribe of twenty manors.
Next he turned upon St. Margaret's, but its
parishioners withstood and drove away his
workmen. Finally, a parish church and three
episcopal residences in the Strand were
seized to provide a site for Somerset House.

The greed of the council rivalled that of
the Protector. Social discontents accentu-
ated religious strife. Wages fell and prices
increased. Townsmen lamented the decline
of trade. Rural folk found that the new
rich, into whose hands had passed the
monastic estates, were unsympathetic and
grasping landlords. It was high time that
the forces of religion should be employed to

lessen, instead of increasing, the troubles of an unhappy people. Papal interference had been bad. Henry's tyranny had been worse. But neither the one nor the other had done so much harm as this misuse of power by a group of unscrupulous and fanatical politicians.

The real need of the Church in those troubled times was a strong and courageous leadership. That Cranmer was unable to supply. Yet he was sincerely anxious to end religious discord, and to provide the English Church with formularies which people of divergent views might agree to accept. He was loth, however, to move by himself. With most of the council he had little sympathy, and he had dared to protest against their confiscation of chantry funds. Common action by the episcopate seemed impossible when it included Gardiner and Latimer, Bonner and Ridley. Therefore he decided to look across the Channel for helpers. With their advice and support, he might hope not only to unite the English Church, but to link together all moderate Protestantism both at home and abroad. Repeated failures had not shaken his faith in the possibility of some such concordat. He invited many foreign divines to cross the sea and to assist him in his task of restoring unity to the English Church.

Most of those whom the Archbishop summoned, and a multitude who were self-invited, were glad to find homes in England. Their own lands had become unsafe for them. In this country under Henry's rule their careers would have been brought to a summary end, but Cranmer made them welcome. Some were given posts of importance. The Regius Professorship of Theology was assigned to Peter Martyr at Oxford, and to Martin Bucer at Cambridge. Others were placed in small cures, or preached to such irregular congregations as they could attract. Switzerland, Germany, France, Spain, and Poland all had representatives among these immigrants. Unless we attribute it to the influence of his marriage, the attraction which these foreign Protestants had for Cranmer seems difficult to explain. The Latin epistles he addressed to them are by far the most cordial of his letters. A group of them clustered about him, and became his intimate counsellors. When a question arose concerning the vestments of an English bishop, it was to a German divine that the Archbishop turned for guidance. It was to the views of German and Swiss

theologians that he deferred most readily
when revising a Prayer-book for the English
Church. It was a German catechism which
he translated as the best means of instructing
English children. Yet this attitude did much
to frustrate his own purpose. A near view
of these pompous and dogmatic foreigners
did not encourage the average Englishman to
accept his religion from their hands. A
growing national spirit had endorsed Henry
VIII.'s breach with Rome. It was not
prepared to transfer its homage from Rome
to Zurich. It held that an Englishman could
form his creed and regulate his Church without interference from outside, and it viewed
with strong disfavour the invasion of English
pulpits by alien sectaries. Even Cranmer
himself found cause to regret some consequences of his action. He had invited
Protestant leaders of the more moderate type,
and with them, whether Calvinists or Zwinglians, his relations were cordial. But upon
their heels came rabid extremists, " anabaptists ", and other eccentric leaders of
eccentric sects. Their violence and lack
of discipline gave the Archbishop endless
trouble, and went far to destroy his scheme
for Protestant union on a large scale.

Among his own countrymen, however, he

hoped to restore peace by providing a book of common worship in their own tongue. The need of it was great. Its value to the Church proved enduring. Yet to suppose that it would promptly end religious differences was what a scholar might dream but no man of affairs would expect. Royal commands, enforced by capital penalties, had attempted the same purpose in the previous reign. Where Henry VIII. had failed, the council of Edward VI. was unlikely to succeed. Passions ran too high, and differences of creed were too fundamental for unity of faith to be achieved by identity of ritual. None the less, Cranmer went forward with his scheme.

With its earlier stages he had busied himself at intervals over a number of years. Probably he had obtained for it the approval of Henry, who himself wrote in 1545 : " We have judged it to be of no small force for the avoiding of strife and contention to have one uniform manner or course of praying throughout our dominions ". A surviving MS., printed in 1915 by the Bradshaw Society under the appropriate title of " Cranmer's Liturgical Projects ", shows that twice at least in Henry's reign the Archbishop was drafting in Latin new forms of Morning and Evening Prayer. They show his willingness to combine materials taken from very different sources—the ancient Sarum offices, the revised Breviary of Cardinal Quignon, and contemporary Lutheran service books. Thus, when the time came for making an English Prayer-book, most of the preparatory work was already done. Even the preface—that now standing second in our Prayer-book, and entitled " Concerning the Service of the Church "—had been written by Cranmer in Latin, and followed closely the Latin preface by Cardinal Quignon. He had only to render his Latin version into English, and the Preface to the first English Prayer-book was complete. The English Litany, as we have noted, was authorised for use in 1545. In March 1548 the Archbishop produced a Communion service, in which the Latin Mass was accompanied by English prayers.

It had no influence upon sectarian quarrels. Month by month they became more bitter. Pulpits were given over to invective, and to invective not only doctrinal but political. Denunciation of heresies merged into open attacks upon the council and its methods. Therefore in April the council forbade all preaching except by certain divines licensed for the purpose. By September even licensed preachers were restricted to delivering printed homilies. The Archbishop and council resolved to hasten the publication of a Prayer-book as the surest means of allaying discord and discontent. In the autumn Cranmer's proposals were reviewed by a committee of bishops. A draft of the book was brought before the House of Lords in December, and provoked a lively debate. On January 21, 1549, the book was authorised by the first Act of Uniformity. After Whitsunday 1549 the use of any other form in public worship was punishable by fine, deprivation, and imprisonment.

Thus, in a time of fierce controversy and national unrest, came into being the Book of Common Prayer. Its tranquil cadences, its noble diction, its spirit of disciplined devotion, have endeared it to generations of our race. No subsequent revisions have altered, or, we may hope, will be permitted to alter, its essential qualities. They are what Cranmer made them in 1549. Indeed, by its retention of prayers used by Englishmen, though in another tongue, through earlier centuries, the book emphasises the continuity of the English Church before, during, and after the Reformation period. But there can be little need to extol at length either the liturgical charm or the historical value of the Prayer-book.

Here we are concerned to remember in how striking a degree we owe them to one man. Against his many failures we can set this triumph. As we follow the sad record of weakness and incompetence, we can rejoice to think that it was Thomas Cranmer who gave us our English Prayer-book, and we shall take this work as his best memorial.

CHAPTER VIII

THROUGH GATHERING CLOUDS

In 1549 the new Prayer-book met with the reception which everyone less simple-minded than its author had foreseen. It was designed to conciliate two parties in sharp conflict. Therefore it was attacked by the extremists of both. It was too Protestant for reactionary Catholics. It was too Catholic for radical Protestants. To all people it brought a change they could not ignore. When they attended their parish churches on Sunday they heard services different in form and language from those to which they and their forefathers had been accustomed. Inevitably, therefore, not only the extremists but folk of moderate views were inclined to be critical. As happens always in such conditions, those who liked the change said little ; those who resented it were loud in expostulation. The Act prescribing its use had menaced with penalties all who should " declare or speak anything in the derogation, depraving, or despising of the same book ", but the threat was commonly ignored. Some attacks were so vehement and others so ribald that after a while the council began to enforce the penal clauses. By that time little remained to be said. Every feature of the book had been discussed from every point of view.

Its sacramental doctrine was, as a whole, far more Catholic than had been expected. Speeches delivered by Cranmer in the House of Lords debate had appeared to indicate his definite conversion to Zwinglianism. The Zwinglian divines in England reported to their brethren in Switzerland the triumph of their cause. All was now over, they added, with the chances of Lutheranism. The greater therefore was their chagrin when they came to examine the Book of Common Prayer. Certainly it could not be termed Lutheran. But yet more definitely it was not Zwinglian. Its dominant note was that of anti-papal Catholicism. The office for " The Supper of the Lord and the Holy Communion, commonly called the Mass " was based on no Protestant formularies but on the ancient liturgy of Sarum. It did not uphold transubstantiation. It did imply unmistakably the doctrine of the Real Presence.

We need not share the surprise of the Zwinglians at this discrepancy between the Archbishop's speeches and the Archbishop's book. Possibly his draft was somewhat modified by the pressure of Catholic peers. Again, even Cranmer's considered writings on Eucharistic doctrine were apt to be confused in their thought and uncertain in their conclusions. Probably enough his spoken words in the House of Lords did not accurately convey his views, or at least the whole of his views. Indeed, his second speech, made after Ridley had taken part in the discussion, somewhat modified his first. But a more important point has to be remembered. Some historians have described the first Prayer-book as " hastily written ", supposing the whole to have been accomplished in the few weeks that intervened between the meeting of bishops and the production of the completed draft. That is to misread the facts. The book was Cranmer's. His preparations for composing it had lasted not merely through a few weeks but over many years. From his Cambridge days he had been keenly interested in liturgical studies. The catalogue of his library shows how wide was his reading in this subject. His MSS. prove that he delighted to compose and translate prayers, to draw up Calendars of holy-days, to plan tables of Scriptural " lessons ". We may be sure that for a long while he had cherished the hope of producing an English Prayer-book. He loved our tongue. He had a most sensitive ear for its cadence and euphony. He developed his gifts by practice and experiment, until he could render the concise and magnificent Latin collects into English nearly as concise and even more magnificent. When in the autumn of 1548 the Prayer-book was to be made, the Archbishop had his notes, schemes, original and translated prayers ready to his hand. His task was to amplify and arrange this material. In this task he had the assistance of his colleagues. But work of the quality which distinguishes the Book of Common Prayer is not hastily improvised in a few weeks.

What, perhaps, he scarcely realised was the rapid change in his theological standpoint since most of these preliminary studies had been completed. Thus it might happen that the Prayer-book represented far more accurately what Cranmer had believed in, we may say, 1543 than what actually he believed at the time of its publication in 1549. This he was driven to realise in a manner as strange as it was unwelcome. No attacks from extreme Catholics or extreme Protestants so angered Cranmer as the praise bestowed on his work by his principal enemy. To Gardiner, still imprisoned in the Tower, the new Prayer-book was shown, in the hope that he would incriminate himself by speaking " in derogation " of it. But he praised what he had been expected to censure. Parts of the book, he said, he would himself have worded differently, but with the whole he was well satisfied. For special eulogy he chose five passages in the Communion service, on the ground that they manifestly upheld the Catholic position. It was a shrewd blow, which sorely discomfited the Archbishop. He and Gardiner were at this time in the thick of their interminable controversy over Eucharistic doctrine. Henceforth Gardiner could cite against Cranmer's arguments the Prayer-book which Cranmer himself had composed; the Prayer-book which was, moreover, the official exposition of the Church's beliefs. The Archbishop was left with no effective reply. He could, and did assert that the meaning attached by Gardiner to these sentences was not that which their author had intended. But he could not deny that the words admitted of Gardiner's inter-

pretation, or even that this was the meaning which every unprejudiced reader would
naturally attach to them.

Therefore Cranmer was stirred to new
action. Attacks on his work might be ignored, but this praise of it was intolerable.
A Prayer-book which pleased Gardiner was
a Prayer-book needing to be re-written. He
began the work at once. He must, as ever,
have some advice on which to lean. His own
colleagues had proved fallible critics. He
turned accordingly to his foreign friends.
Martyr and Bucer were invited to suggest
emendations from the Protestant standpoint.
When in 1552 the second Prayer-book was
published, each of the passages welcomed by
Gardiner had been modified. Possibly there
might have been no Prayer-book of 1552 had
not Gardiner applauded the Prayer-book of
1549.

Cranmer's dream of an England pacified
and united by the new Prayer-book quickly
proved vain. In 1549 public affairs went from
bad to worse. In March much feeling was
stirred by the execution of Thomas Seymour,
lord high admiral, brother of the Protector.
His character cannot be defended. He was
shameless alike in his neglect of public duties
and in his pursuit of private gain. For

political reasons he had married Henry VIII.'s widow, and after her demise paid court to the Princess Elizabeth. That he was guilty of treasonable intrigue appears certain. Yet imprisonment would have made him harmless, and the capital sentence passed on him seemed to savour of fratricide. The revulsion against it was the more pronounced because the Archbishop of Canterbury was known, in defiance of canon law, to have affixed his signature to the death warrant. This was a deed which Cranmer's habitual weakness can explain but cannot excuse.

During the summer serious risings against the council broke out in the east, south, and west of England. Considerable force and the use of hired troops from Germany and Italy were needed to suppress them. In the east and south they were political and agrarian. Dislike of the government was linked with hatred of the rich property-owners, who were enclosing land, putting it out of cultivation, and diminishing employment. But in Devon and Cornwall the uprising was due to religious grievances, and, in particular, to the enforcement of the new Prayer-book. Violent altercations took place during the time of service. Before long the insurgents numbered many thousands. Exeter was besieged for six

weeks. The rebels drew up a formal pre-
sentment of their complaints, in fifteen
" Articles ". Cranmer wrote a full and
forcible reply. He assumed that they were
not the work of the " peasants " on whose
behalf they were put forward, but of " subtle
and wily papistical traitors ", who " devised
these Articles for you ". That a large number
of the rustic folk preferred the old services to
the new and were ready to revolt was true
enough. But Cranmer was plainly right in
attributing the Articles to other sources. One
demanded the re-enactment of the Statute of
Six Articles. Another asked for the recall of
the banished Cardinal Pole. Such matters
would hardly be the genuine grievances of
villagers in Devon and Cornwall. The real
instigators of these petitions were west-
country squires and clergy of Romanist
sympathies. Among other points desired
were the mass in Latin and without communicants, communion in one kind, the host hung
over the high altar for worship, the doctrine
of purgatory to be preached, English Bibles
to be forbidden, and the new Prayer-book to
be withdrawn.

The Archbishop dealt trenchantly with
each Article in turn. The eighth ran :

We will not receive the new service, because it is

but like a Christmas game ; but we will have our old service of matins, mass, evensong, and procession (*i.e.* litany) in Latin, as it was before. And so we the Cornish men, whereof certain of us understand no English, utterly refuse this new English.

The comparison with " a Christmas game " is obscure, but may be due to the frequent changes of posture—standing, sitting, and kneeling—prescribed in the rubrics of the Prayer-book. " It is more like a game," retorted Cranmer, " and a fond play to be laughed at of all men to hear the priest speak aloud to the people in Latin . . . and many times the thing that the priest saith in Latin is so fond of itself, that it is more like a play than a godly prayer." His rejoinder to the second sentence of the Article is effective enough :

I would gladly know the reason why the Cornish men refuse utterly the new English, as you call it, because certain of you understand it not ; and yet you will have the service in Latin, which almost none of you understand. If this be a sufficient cause for Cornwall to refuse the English service, because some of you understand none English, a much greater cause have they, both of Cornwall and Devonshire, to refuse utterly the late service ; forasmuch as fewer of them know the Latin tongue than they of Cornwall the English tongue.

A demand which probably represented the genuine wish of the countryside was for the re-establishment of religious houses and the restoration of their ownership of half the monastic properties. One Article, with no reference to religion, perhaps expressed the grievance of farmers who found that their labourers were being drawn away into gentle-folk's service :

We will that no gentleman shall have any mo (more) servants than one to wait upon him, except he may dispend one hundred mark land. And for every hundred mark we think it reasonable he should have a man.

Cranmer's answer to this is particularly vigorous :

Yet have you not foreseen one thing, you wise dispensers of the commonwealth. For if a gentle-man of an hundred mark land (who by your order must have but one servant, except he might spend two hundred marks) should send that one servant to London, you have not provided who shall wait upon him until his servant come home again. Nor have you provided where every gentleman may have one servant who can do all things necessary for him. I fear me the most part of you that devised this Article (whom I take to be loiterers and idle un-thrifts), if you should serve a gentleman, he would be fain to do all things himself, for any thing that you could or would do for him. . . . For was it ever seen in any country since the world began that the commons did appoint the nobles and gentlemen the number of their servants ? Standeth it with any reason to turn upside down the good order of the whole world, that is everywhere, and ever hath been?

. . . Will you now have the subjects to govern their king, the villains to rule the gentlemen, and the servants their masters ? If men would suffer this, God will not. . . .

But it was by force of arms, not by Cranmer's arguments, that the western rising was ultimately subdued. This revolt alarmed the council beyond any other. Its Romanist colour made them suspect that its real instigators were the Princess Mary and her friends. The suspicion was unfounded, but the fear of Mary was natural enough. She flouted the authority of the council, and disregarded both blandishment and threats. Her chaplains still celebrated mass, and private baptisms according to the Latin rite were performed in her house. Lengthy remonstrances, evidently from Cranmer's pen, were sent her by the council. Her reply was decisive :

Though you have forgotten the king my father, yet both God's commandment and nature will not suffer me to do so. Wherefore, with God's help, I will remain an obedient child to his laws, as he left them, till such time as the king's majesty my brother shall have perfect years of discretion.

In the autumn of 1549 the hopes of Romanists and Catholics revived. With untiring industry and malign skill the Earl of Warwick had plotted to bring about the

Protector's downfall. In September he succeeded. Somerset was imprisoned. The
Protectorate came to an end. Warwick, soon
to be created Duke of Northumberland,
obtained the leadership of the council.
Because he had been foremost in crushing
the social revolution, he was expected to
oppose the religious revolution also. Mass
was promptly restored in college chapels, and
Gardiner and Bonner counted on release.
Yet it soon became clear that the expected
reaction was not to come. Northumberland
himself had no religious feelings. Having
used Catholic assistance in gaining his
supremacy, he decided to use Protestant
support in retaining it. Catholic nobles who
had aided him in procuring the downfall of
Somerset were pushed contemptuously aside
when this purpose had been achieved. In
the council itself the Protestant faction was
still supreme. In order to reinforce it,
Somerset after a while was released from
prison and allowed to have a seat at the table.
Such influence as Cranmer had been able to
exercise in the days of the Protectorate
diminished rapidly when Northumberland
became the ruler of England. This, so far as
it resulted from Northumberland's personal
dislike of Cranmer, was to the Archbishop's

credit.   Somerset was incapable and foolish
enough, yet it was possible to feel some sort
of respect for him as a quite sincere fanatic.
But to respect Northumberland, or to live on
terms of friendship with him, was not possible
for any man of decent principles.

We cannot blame Cranmer because his
voice counted for little in public affairs when
public affairs were dominated by Northumberland.   Yet he alienated also the sympathies of Englishmen with no extreme
religious or political views by his strange
infatuation for foreigners.   At his encouragement they continued to flock into this
country.   A congregation of them were
granted a church of their own in London,
under the charge of John à Lasco, a learned
Pole.   Another colony of foreign Protestants
was allowed, with strange incongruity, to
establish itself beside the ruined but hallowed
walls of Glastonbury.   The mere presence of
such immigrants might have been inoffensive
in itself.   What did not seem inoffensive was
their assumption of a mission to transform the
English Church to their own liking, to decide
what the English Prayer-book should contain, and what ritual should or should not
be permitted in English worship.   Englishmen grew resentful when this arrogance was

encouraged, and even invited, by the Archbishop of Canterbury.

The council's dealings with the episcopate proved that the official policy was to be more aggressively Protestant under Northumberland than it had been under Somerset. Bonner was not only still imprisoned but deprived of his see. In 1551 Gardiner was deprived of Winchester, Heath of Worcester, Day of Chichester. In 1552 the scholarly and gentle Tunstall was ejected from Durham and sent to the Tower, on a charge so patently absurd that even Cranmer was moved to protest. Men of extreme Protestant views were chosen to fill the sees vacant by deprivations. Nicholas Ridley, on whom Bonner's diocese of London was bestowed, found his clergy still inclined to " counterfeit the popish mass ". The surest way of thwarting them, he felt, would be to replace the altar by " an honest table, decently covered ". Accordingly he enjoined the destruction of altars throughout his diocese, and himself superintended the overthrow of the high altar in St. Paul's. So welcome to the council was this action, that they commanded the bishops of all dioceses to follow Ridley's example. They were also to preach sermons on the subject, and were supplied with headings for their sermons. The circular letter was signed by Cranmer, among others, and the not very convincing sermon-notes were probably from his pen. The vast damage already inflicted on ancient churches by the destruction of " images " was increased by this new ordinance ; much exquisite wood-work and embroidery perished with the altars themselves.

Militant, however, as was the Protestantism of Ridley, it did not equal that of the man nominated to the see of Gloucester. If Ridley were what in modern parlance would be termed an extreme Low Churchman, John Hooper could scarcely be accounted a Churchman at all. Indeed, he has been described as " the father of English Non-conformity ", and the title is not ill-deserved. A monk in his early days, he had afterwards transferred his allegiance to the most thorough-going of the Swiss reformers. He had no wish for a bishopric. The oath he would be required to take seemed to him impious, and the episcopal vestments he considered super-stitious and popish. Most properly, there-fore, he declined the appointment. The council would not accept his refusal. As argument failed to move him, they deter-mined to try other means, and fell back on

the strange expedient of committing him to
prison until he should consent to be made a
bishop.   After a few weeks of confinement,
Hooper withdrew his objections, and was
consecrated Bishop of Gloucester.

The council's dealings with the episcopate were matched by their treatment of
the parochial clergy.   Those suspected of
Catholic leanings were ejected.   Too often
the vacancies were left unfilled, and the
incomes transferred by lay patrons to their
own pockets.   When an incumbent was at
length provided, not improbably he was one
of the patron's servants, nominated on condition that he made over all but a fraction
of the revenue to his master.   So common
became this scandal, that special legislation
was found necessary to check it.   Episcopal
authority was seldom exercised and yet more
seldom obeyed.   A large proportion of the
clergy were unfit for their work both in
morals and learning.   Even Hooper was
shocked to find 168 priests in his diocese who
were unable to recite the Ten Command-
ments.   The illiteracy of the clergy in 1552
may be attributed in a large measure to
the decline of the universities through the
previous decade.   Between 1542 and 1548
only 191 men were admitted to the B.A.

degree at Cambridge, and 173 at Oxford. In 1549 Latimer complained, in a sermon preached before the king, that " there be none now but great men's sons in colleges, and their fathers look not to have them preachers ". The council and their friends pilfered endowments meant to encourage religious learning. In 1551 the Master of St. John's College roundly declared that the greed of one courtier was worse than that " of fifty tun-bellied monks ". Thus the people of England lacked guidance and instruction from competent clergy at the time when it was most needed. Religious controversies formed the common talk, and from talk the disputants passed often to blows. Ale-house tipplers wrangled over the Eucharist, and the Sunday services were interrupted by fights that would not have been tolerated in an ale-house. The repute of the Church was brought low indeed. Cranmer could do little to check this degeneracy. That he felt it acutely we need not doubt. His secretary, Morice, tells us that

to the face of the world his countenance, diet, or sleep never altered or changed, so that they which were most near and conversant about him never or seldom perceived by no sign or token of countenance how the affairs of the prince or the realm went. Notwithstanding, with his secret and special friends he would shed forth many bitter tears, lamenting the miseries and calamities of the world.

Miserable and calamitous are epithets that justly describe the state of England and of England's Church in the reign of Edward VI.

At the beginning of 1552 Northumberland achieved the full purpose of his ambition. To secure his own supremacy at the council he had contrived the fall and imprisonment of Somerset. To gain the Protestant support he needed, he had released Somerset and readmitted him to the council. But Somerset was still a rival, and a rival who might become dangerous. Despite his faults, he had a hold on the populace, and the populace detested Northumberland. Therefore Somerset was again arrested, brought to trial, and executed. His death made Northumberland secure. One further step was necessary to complete his plan. He insisted that, though the technical regency of the council must continue, in fact the king was now competent to rule. Then he himself secured absolute domination over that precocious but sickly child. The royal actions were what Northumberland willed. Henceforward Northumberland was virtually king of England, with Edward for his mouthpiece.

With the attainment of his ambition passed

the need of conciliating any one. In particular he troubled no longer to disguise his hatred of the Archbishop, who had refused to connive at some of his most shameful peculations. Cranmer doubtless spoke the truth when he declared afterwards to Mary that the Duke had been " seeking long time my destruction ". Lest he should give his enemy the handle he sought, Cranmer ceased to attend meetings of the council. Through the remainder of this reign he lived mostly in seclusion in Canterbury. An interesting sketch of his daily routine has come down to us ; the work, probably, of his faithful friend and secretary. The Archbishop rose at five, and spent his time until nine in study and prayer. From nine until the hour of dinner he interviewed callers and dealt with his official correspondence. After dinner, " for an hour or thereabouts he would play at the chess, or behold such as could play ". We may suspect that he won but few games, that his strategy was irresolute, and that he was lured easily into traps set by an astute opponent. Yet it is interesting to know that Cranmer was of that great company who have found in playing, or even in watching, chess a real solace and refreshment of the mind. When board and men had been put away, he returned to his study and literary work until five, when he heard evensong. After that, he walked or " used some honest pastime " until supper. For supper too often he had no appetite, yet he never failed to take his place at the table. As a rule, he had a number of guests at this meal, whom he entertained with " such fruitful talk as did repask and much delight the hearers ". After supper he allowed himself another hour of " walking or some other honest pastime ". Then he returned to his study again until nine o'clock. And so to bed.

Many of these long hours were spent upon compositions designed to restore religious peace. One such task was the revision of the Prayer-book. In making this Cranmer sought the help of the Bishops of London and Ely, while paying special attention also to the criticisms of the foreign divines. But Convocation was given no part in the business, nor was its approval sought for the completed work. In January 1552 a second Act of Uniformity authorised the use of the new Prayer-book, yet it was not actually printed for another nine months, during which further modifications were made in the draft. When it appeared, the variations from the Book of

1549 were found to be very numerous. Some, such as the addition of the exhortation, confession, and absolution to matins, had no marked doctrinal significance. Others, however, were plainly intended to conciliate the Protestants. Eucharistic vestments were forbidden. The words " mass " and " altar " were disused. Reservation of the sacrament, for whatever purpose, was prohibited. Intercession for the departed was struck out from the Prayer for the Church. Most significant of all was the change in the words of administration. In the 1549 Book they consisted of the first part only of the form as we know it to-day. In the 1552 Book they consisted of the second part only. In place of " The Body of our Lord Jesus Christ ", etc., was substituted " Take and eat this in remembrance ", etc., with a corresponding change at the administration of the chalice. In the subsequent revision of Elizabeth's reign the two sentences, by an admirable compromise characteristic of the English habit, were conjoined. At the same time a commemoration of the faithful departed was restored, though in a modified form, to the Prayer for the Church. It is clear that by removing all mention of the Body and Blood of our Lord from the words of administration, and by substituting " Take and eat this in remembrance . . . feed upon Him in thy heart " ; " Drink this in remembrance ", Cranmer hoped to have evolved a form which those who believed in the Real Presence might accept, and those who did not believe would welcome.

Of his practical success or failure we can scarcely judge. This Second Prayer-book was legally in use for no more than eight months, and practically by many parishes was never used at all. Moreover, it never received the Church's approval through a vote of Convocation. Yet in justice to Cranmer we must recollect that his work, if less Catholic than the Catholics desired, was also less Protestant than the Protestants demanded. At this time he was driven to realise that the extreme Protestant ideas, if allowed full scope, would not so much reform the historic Church as transform it into a new body. Great pressure to admit such changes into the Prayer-book was put upon him between January and October 1552 by Northumberland and the council. But he stood firm. He cannot be blamed for one unauthorised addition, made at the last moment. Among the few divines favoured by Northumberland was John Knox, whom he brought south to be " a whetstone, to quicken and sharp the Bishop of Canterbury, whereof he hath need ". In a sermon at court Knox vehemently assailed the practice of kneeling at the reception of Holy Communion. Hooper had already denounced the custom, in characteristic language, as " grievous and damnable idolatry ". Thereupon the council urged the Archbishop to order in his new Prayer-book that communicants must sit or stand at the time of reception. Cranmer replied :

My good lordships, I pray you to consider that there be two prayers which go before the receiving of the Sacrament, and two immediately follow, all which time the people, praying and giving thanks, do kneel. . . . If the kneeling of the people should be discontinued at the receiving of the Sacrament, so that at the receipt thereof they should rise up and stand or sit, and then immediately kneel down again, it should rather import a contemptuous than a reverent receiving of the Sacrament. . . .

Rebuffed on this point, the council decided to act on their own initiative. They sent a hurried message to the printer forbidding him to distribute copies of the Prayer-book until an additional note had been supplied to the service of Holy Communion. As the printing was already finished, this had to appear on a fly-leaf. It was the " declaration on kneeling ", which became commonly known as " the black rubric ". It was designed to show that the act of kneeling implies no adoration of the consecrated elements. As originally worded, it denied " the real and essential Presence " of Christ in the Sacrament ; a phrase significantly altered to " the corporal Presence " in the seventeenth century.

Together with the making of a new Prayer-book, Cranmer busied himself with other projects for ecclesiastical settlement. The most ambitious was a complete re-drafting of the canon law. A large company of divines assisted him in framing his elaborate proposals. Perhaps their most striking feature was the transference to diocesan synods of functions exercised previously by Convocation. But the opposition of Northumberland brought the whole scheme to the ground.

Yet neither this nor any other disappointment shook Cranmer's faith in his fixed idea. He saw that Church and State alike were torn by religious dissension. He saw how greatly the ending of this strife was to be desired. He was sure that it would be ended, and ended promptly, by the publication of some formulary which men of differing beliefs could accept. In Henry's reign neither the Ten Articles nor the Six had succeeded. In Edward's the First Prayer-book had failed ;

the chance of the Second was doubtful. But Cranmer had another resource in store. Preachers seeking a licence in his diocese were required to sign a set of Articles prepared by himself. So far as he knew, these preachers lived at peace with one another. Might not the same specific, applied on a larger scale, achieve results of wider beneficence? He had found a friend at court in Sir William Cecil, now the king's secretary. To Cecil he sent his Articles. He hoped that the king would command the bishops, and the bishops their clergy, to subscribe them. "And then," he told Cecil, with unextinguishable optimism, "I trust that such a concord and quiet shall shortly follow thereof, as else is not to be looked for for many years."

He had to wait seven months for the granting of his request. Then, in June 1553, his Articles of Religion, considerably emended and reduced in number from forty-five to forty-two, were issued by the council in the king's name. The statement of their title-page that they had been accepted by Convocation was entirely false. Their chief interest lies in the fact that they were the basis of those Thirty-nine Articles which, authorised under Elizabeth, are still retained by our Church. Their character is more readily understood when their original purpose is remembered. Most negotiators would try first to obtain agreement on controverted matters and then signatures to articles embodying that agreement. Such was not Cranmer's method. He was sanguine that if signatures could be obtained agreement would follow. In order to make signature easy, his Articles were as indeterminate as possible. Necessarily they fixed certain limits of conformity and insisted on certain truths. Within such limits they could be intentionally vague. If one part of a sentence so exactly balanced the next that the whole was ambiguous, so much the better. If an Article were so phrased that a Catholic could interpret it in one sense, a Protestant in another, that was sheer gain. Both would sign it, and thereafter both would live in peace. Such was Cranmer's theory. It has been forgotten often by disputants looking to the Articles for precise statements of doctrine. Not identity of belief but comprehensiveness was the end which the Articles of Religion were designed to achieve.

Their immediate result was not what Cranmer hoped. So far from bestowing " quiet and concord ", they stirred new dissension. But the religious history of England was about to be changed by an event more

potent than the issue of Articles. When
Edward signed them on June 12, 1553, he was
already ill beyond hope of recovery. Northumberland felt his own plight to be desperate.
He had no mind to surrender the virtual
kingship he had gained. Indeed, he could
scarcely surrender it and hope to live. His
friends were few and discredited. Like
Somerset, he was hated by his fellow-nobles.
Unlike Somerset, he was loathed by the
populace. Yet he would be still secure and
still supreme if Edward's successor were his
daughter - in - law. He had arranged a
marriage between his fourth son and Lady
Jane Grey. Then he persuaded the dying
boy, by pleading that thus only could Protestantism be saved, to set aside his father's
will, to make a wholly illegal use of his prerogative, and to transfer to Lady Jane Grey the
succession. When the judges were bidden
to sign the document embodying this nefarious
scheme, they protested that signature was
treason. Only when they had sheltered themselves by a special commission and an advance
pardon did they yield. Even then one of
their number, Sir James Hales, had the
courage to refuse.

Next came the turn of the council.
Cranmer was told to add his signature to the

others.   He argued, he pleaded, he demurred, he hesitated.   Had the request been made to him in writing, we can conceive how definite and vigorous would have been his refusal.   But, as ever, he was incapable of holding his ground when face to face with resolute opponents.   His lamentable weakness prevailed, and he signed.

It was an act, indeed, not merely of cowardice but of treason and perjury.   Impartial history cannot attempt to justify it. Defences have been attempted by at least two biographers of Cranmer, of whom one wrote to eulogise him as a bulwark of Catholicism against Protestantism, the other as a leader of Protestantism against Catholicism.   Both, in their wish to magnify his character, hold that he did no serious wrong by yielding to Northumberland.   Both require us to believe that faults reprehensible in a man of the world are venial in a pious archbishop.   The best that can be said for Cranmer is that he admitted the true quality of his action when he was seeking to escape its penalties.   Lest we seem to judge him too harshly, let us hear what he himself can urge in extenuation when he asks of Mary

mercy and pardon for my heinous folly and offence, in consenting and following the testament and last will of our late sovereign ; which will, God he knoweth, I never liked ; nor never anything grieved me so much that your grace's brother did. And if by any means it had been in me to have letted the making of that will, I would have done it. And what I said therein, as well to the council as himself, divers of your majesty's council can report ; but none so well as the marquis of Northampton and the lord Darcy ; which two were present at the communication between the king's majesty and me. I desired to talk with the king's majesty alone, but I could not be suffered, and so I failed of my purpose. For if I might have communed with the king alone, and at good leisure, my trust was, that I should have altered him from that purpose ; but, they being present, my labour was vain.

Then when I could not dissuade him from the said will, and both he and his privy council informed me that the judges and his learned counsel said that the act of entailing the crown, made by his father, could not be prejudicial to him, but that he, being in possession of the crown, might make his will thereof ; this seemed very strange unto me. But being the sentence of his judges and other his learned counsel, methought it became not me, being unlearned in the law, to stand against my prince therein. And so at length I was required by the king's majesty himself to set my hand to the will ; saying, that he trusted I alone would not be more repugnant to his will than the rest of the council were : (which words surely grieved my heart very sore) and so I granted him to subscribe his will, and to follow the same.

What were the facts ?   On his own state-ment, Cranmer " never liked " the will.   He forgot to add that, like it or not, he could not endorse it without perjury. He had been the favoured and devoted servant of Henry VIII. At his deathbed he had sworn to accept and uphold Henry's will, which Edward's set aside. Cranmer was by no means, as he averred, " unlearned in the law ", and no skilled knowledge of it was needed to reveal the flagrant illegality of Edward's action. So far from uttering the opinion Cranmer attributed to them, the " judges and other learned counsel " had said emphatically that signature would be treason. A question to any of them would have verified this fact. By his own confession, the Primate, a man of sixty-three, defied his conscience in order to oblige a fevered boy of fifteen. Moreover, he knew under whose influence Edward made his request. He knew what would be the results to England of granting it. He knew that it would bestow a new lease of power upon Northumberland, and he knew Northumberland for the un-principled ruffian he was. Yet Cranmer perjured himself and signed. His own term, " heinous folly and offence ", certainly was none too strong for a deed so unworthy of his office and his better self.

On July 6 Edward died. On the 10th Lady Jane Grey was proclaimed queen.

On the 18th she wrote a pathetic appeal for aid, " given under our signet at our Tower of London, the first year of our reign ". Within a few days her palace became her prison, which she was to leave only by its scaffold. On the 21st Northumberland was under arrest. His scheme had ignored public opinion. Mismanagement, corruption, anarchy, heavy taxation, civil and religious strife, social misery, had been the fruits of his rule. Of Northumberland and Protestantism England was resolved to be rid. On August 3 Mary entered London as queen, and was welcomed with passionate enthusiasm.

CHAPTER IX

THE END

THE persecutions that made Mary's reign infamous had no place in its beginning. Through its first six months her attitude towards religious questions was in doubt. That Protestantism had fallen was indeed certain. The national spirit which had enabled her father to overthrow the papal power now exulted in the flight of foreign Protestants. At least eight hundred hastened across the sea, taking with them five bishops and other Englishmen who had accepted their doctrines. They felt that Strassburg, Frankfort, Basle, or Geneva would be a safer place of residence than England under Mary Tudor.

When this party had fallen, however, two others remained, and for a time no man could say which would be given royal support. On the one side were the Romanists, who still favoured the papal claims, and hated alike the changes made by Henry and by Edward. On the other were the anti-papal Catholics, whose point of view was represented by the First Prayer-book. They were led by Gardiner, who at the beginning of the reign emerged from prison to become Chancellor and chief adviser of the queen. He hoped that she would maintain England's independence of the papacy, marry an Englishman, and accept the moderate Reformation principles reached at the close of Henry's reign. For a time it seemed likely that his hopes might be fulfilled. Mary showed unexpected tolerance, and granted pardons liberally. Legislation of the previous reign was undone, but the repealing statutes made no reference to papal supremacy, and in fact the title of " Supreme Head " was still used by the queen. Unhappily for Mary and for England, Gardiner's counsel was set aside. Soon it became clear that Romanism, not anti-papal Catholicism, was to prevail. If Mary was the daughter of a king who, with all his faults, was an English patriot, she was the daughter also of a Spanish princess. Her sympathies were Spanish, and she resolved to wed Philip of Spain. No other choice could have extinguished so completely the national enthusiasm which had welcomed her accession. It would place the country under the double thrall of a Spanish consort and the Pope. It furnished the Protestants with an excuse for armed revolt. And it placed Gardiner, with all who had supported the Reformation under Henry, in a cruel dilemma. They had no relish either for the rule of Rome or for the doctrines of Geneva. If they submitted to Mary, it was because they preferred to figure as Roman Catholics rather than cease to be Catholics at all.

The following years witnessed a hideous persecution. Not Pole, or Bonner, or Spanish friars, but Mary herself was its instigator. All that can be said in her defence is that her mind was unhinged. Deserted by her husband and disappointed of a child, physiological and mental derangement made her attribute all her woes to divine wrath, and divine wrath was only to be appeased by holocausts of heretics. What she did ensure was that a creed in the name of which three hundred persons were burnt within four years would not be the religion of the English people.

For six weeks after the queen's arrival in London Cranmer was left at large. Some writers have applauded his courage in refusing to use a supposed opportunity of flight.

In fact there was no opportunity. The ports were closely watched. Even an eminent foreigner like Martyr could not cross the sea until he had obtained a special passport from the queen. No doubt less conspicuous Protestants were allowed, or even encouraged, to escape, while pardons were granted to those who had taken a minor share in Northumberland's conspiracy. But Northumberland was in the Tower, and his chief confederates, among whom Cranmer was reckoned, were kept under close surveillance until a time convenient for their trial should arrive. Cranmer realised his extreme peril. He knew himself to be guilty of treason. He knew how little cause he had to expect clemency, having stigmatised the queen's mother as an adulteress and herself as a bastard. He had wrecked Katharine's life. He had persecuted Mary in her youth that she might declare herself illegitimate. To the end he had defamed her mother and derided her religion. Even recently he had sent her, on behalf of Edward's council, a letter strangely insolent. Very different was to be his next letter, in which, "most lamentably mourning and moaning himself unto your highness, Thomas Cranmer, although unworthy himself either to write or speak unto your highness ", sued for pardon. That Cranmer in these circumstances, and with the charge of treason hanging over him, should go out of his way to stir afresh Mary's anger against him, must seem an act of almost incredible folly.

Such an act, nevertheless, Cranmer committed. As is inevitable in times of crisis, London seethed with rumours. One of the most improbable was that Cranmer had reintroduced the mass at Canterbury—which in fact had been done by Thornden, suffragan Bishop of Dover—and was shortly to celebrate it, according to the unreformed rite, in the presence of the queen. He might have left the story to falsify itself. He might have met it with a simple denial. What he did was to compose a fierce manifesto, describing the Bishop of Dover as " a false, flattering, lying, and dissembling monk ", and adding that the mass " containeth many horrible blasphemies ". His foolish friend Scory, lately Bishop of Chichester, declaimed this composition in Cheapside. Copies were distributed widely. However disposed to clemency Mary might be, she could not ignore a public statement from the Archbishop of Canterbury that her religion was based on horrible blasphemies. On September 13 Cranmer

was summoned before the council.   On the
next day he was committed to the Tower.
He was never to know liberty again.

Two months later, on November 13, with
Lady Jane Grey and three sons of Northumberland, he was brought to trial at the
Guildhall on the charge of treason.   All the
prisoners pleaded guilty, and all were condemned to death.   Parliament confirmed the
sentence.   Having been attainted of treason,
Cranmer was automatically made incapable
of holding office.   Henceforward he was described as "late Archbishop of Canterbury",
and the Primacy remained vacant for the next
three years.   That the capital sentence pronounced on him was technically just is indis-
putable.   But personal inclination, political
expediency, or a union of the two motives,
restrained Mary from permitting it to take
effect.   Cranmer's petition for forgiveness
was ignored, yet for his undoubted treason he
had to suffer no worse penalty than imprisonment.   He was confined again in the Tower,
to which Ridley and Latimer already had
been committed.   The three were lodged in
one room, and beguiled the time with New
Testament study.   They were there still
when, in February 1554, the Tower witnessed
one of the foulest crimes ever perpetrated in

the name of justice. Wyatt's futile rebellion was used as a pretext for beheading Lady Jane Grey, who had not yet reached her seventeenth year. Guildford Dudley, her husband, suffered with her. Cranmer again escaped. Perhaps the queen had decided already that he who had assailed her as a papist should be punished not as a traitor but as a heretic.

Towards this a step was taken in the following month. In his attack upon the mass Cranmer had expressed a wish to champion his sacramental views in public debate. The wish was to be fulfilled, though in a setting he little desired. Convocation appointed its prolocutor and seven divines to dispute with Cranmer, Ridley, and Latimer. To these seven divines were joined seven from Oxford and seven from Cambridge. The instrument nominating the Cambridge delegates shows plainly that the issue was prejudged. They were not to hold an impartial inquiry, but to expose and condemn the three bishops as " sons of iniquity and perdition, and seditious innovators of error ".

The commission was to sit in Oxford. In March therefore the three prisoners were removed from the Tower to Bocardo, the common gaol of Oxford, and on Saturday,

Q

April 14, the proceedings began. The twenty-one divines, with Dr. Weston, prolocutor, as their president, took their seats before the high altar of St. Mary's Church. A pyx hung above them. Cranmer was brought before them in the custody of the mayor of Oxford. He was handed a paper containing " articles " of sacramental doctrine, framed by the doctors, and told that on the following Monday he was either to accept or dispute them. To dispute he was very willing. In his own academic days he had taken part in or presided over many such discussions. Every postulant for a doctor's degree had publicly to debate a thesis with an opponent selected for the purpose, while the other doctors listened, and ultimately sanctioned the degree if the candidate had maintained his cause with adequate ability. Cranmer himself was a most skilful debater, with wide learning, swift perception of weakness in an adversary's case, and a ready, if too copious, power of speech.

But on the Monday the formal disputation soon degenerated into a wrangle. The twenty-one divines were not willing to allow one of their number to argue while the rest listened. All of them insisted on breaking into the debate. The prolocutor was impatient and ill-tempered. Cranmer was like a swordsman who had expected a fencing match with a single opponent while umpires watched, and found himself instead plunged into a general *mêlée*. He described the experience vividly enough in a letter to the council :

This is to signify your lordships that upon Monday, Tuesday, and Wednesday last past were open disputations here in Oxford against me, Master Ridley, and Master Latimer, in three matters concerning the Sacrament : first, of the Real Presence ; secondly, of transubstantiation ; and thirdly, of the sacrifice of the mass. How the other two were used, I cannot tell ; for we were separated, so that none of us knew what the other said, nor how they were ordered. But as concerning myself, I can report that I never knew nor heard of a more confused disputation in all my life. For albeit there was one appointed to dispute against me, yet every man spake his mind, and brought forth what him liked without order. And such haste was made, that no answer could be suffered to be given fully to any argument before another brought a new argument. And in such weighty and large matters there was no remedy but the disputations must be ended in one day which can scantly well be ended in three months ! . . .

On the Thursday, however, Cranmer obtained some small consolation. An unfortunate Oxford candidate for a degree was put up to dispute with him, and Cranmer triumphed with the ease of a practised fencer disarming a novice. But throughout the doctors admired his learning and praised his moderation. Ridley was more vituperative. Latimer was too old and ill to argue. Such details, however, were immaterial. The result had been determined in advance, and on the Friday all three were formally declared to be heretics. No penal consequences followed, for as yet the heresy laws of Henry VIII., repealed under Edward, had not been re-enacted. Through another weary period of almost eighteen months Cranmer, Ridley, and Latimer remained in the Oxford gaol.

They were months of sinister omen for prisoners convicted of heresy. In the course of them Mary wedded Philip of Spain. Spanish friars arrived to teach Englishmen the methods of the Inquisition. Cardinal Pole, whose simpering affectations failed to conceal his malicious cruelty, was welcomed by the queen as papal legate. The heresy laws were revived and put into operation. Early in 1555 the burnings began. In that year not fewer than seventy-five victims were sent to the stake. Now that death in this hideous form, and no mere loss of freedom, was to be the penalty of differing from the papal creed, now that heretics were to be not merely prosecuted but persecuted, it became clear that the late Primate, of all heretics best known to the world and most hated by the queen, could not hope for continued respite.

In September the blow fell. Cranmer received a formal citation to appear at Rome within eighty days, but was also told that the hearing of his case had been delegated to Brooks, Bishop of Gloucester, and would be taken forthwith. His trial opened in the University Church of Oxford on September 12. The Dean of St. Paul's and the Archdeacon of Canterbury were joined with Brooks to hear it. The charges against Cranmer were set out under sixteen heads, but ultimately resolved themselves into three : that he had violated the law of clerical celibacy, that he had written in denial of transubstantiation, and that he had broken his consecration oath of obedience to the papacy. In effect, then, he was charged with adultery, heresy, and perjury. For answer he was content to deny the papal jurisdiction, and consequently that of Brooks, its representative. The facts admitted of little dispute, and his case was vulnerable enough from the forensic standpoint. It must be admitted that he appeared to little advantage under the ruthless crossexamination of Dr. Martin, the queen's proctor. At the close Brooks forwarded a report of the trial to Rome, for the Pope's judgment. No one could doubt what it would be.

Cranmer himself knew well enough. Yet for the moment he showed resolute courage. In a letter to the queen he set down at length the speech he had made before Brooks. He was aware that its language about the Pope would but increase his peril. " I have not spoken it," he said, " for fear of punishment, and to avoid the same, thinking it rather an occasion to aggravate than to diminish my trouble. But I have spoken it from my most bounden duty to the Crown, liberties, laws, and customs of this realm of England." He protested against a form of proceeding which made the king and queen his prosecutors and the Pope his judge :

as though the king and queen could not do or have justice within their own realm against their own subjects, but they must seek it at a stranger's hands. . . . I would have wished to have had some meaner adversaries ; and I think that death shall not grieve me much more than to have had my most dread and most gracious sovereign lord and lady (to whom, under God, I do owe all obedience) to be mine accusers in judgment within their own realm before any stranger and outward power.

It was a shrewd point, skilfully phrased. Yet Mary had not acted without weighing her actions. She desired to put beyond question the supremacy of the Pope over the English Church. It would be demonstrated in dramatic fashion when an Archbishop of Canterbury was executed for heresy by order of the Bishop of Rome.

Cranmer's next sentence illustrates his characteristic blindness to blots on his own record :

Forasmuch as in the time of the prince of most famous memory, King Henry VIII., your grace's father, I was sworn never to consent that the bishop of Rome should exercise any authority or jurisdiction in this realm of England, therefore, lest I should allow his authority contrary to mine oath, I refused to make answer to the bishop of Gloucester, sitting here in judgment by the Pope's authority, lest I should run into perjury.

Mary's rejoinder, had she cared to make it, was obvious enough. She could have remarked that dread of perjury had not deterred Cranmer from violating Henry's will, which he had sworn to uphold. And she might have added that if he had taken an oath of allegiance to Henry, he had taken also an oath of obedience to the Pope. What she did, however, was to place Cranmer's document in the hands of Pole. From Pole some weeks later came a reply of inordinate length, the laboured sophistries of which did not mask his malicious triumph over a doomed foe.

The weeks and months dragged on. With Ridley and Latimer, as men of less importance, the papal legate could deal, and their case was not remitted to Rome. They were bidden to recant, and refused. On October 16 they were burnt, meeting death with heroic fortitude. Cranmer was made to witness their sufferings. That ghastly spectacle, the strain of more than two years' imprisonment, grave illness of body, and the natural infirmity of his mind, all united to shake the courage shown in his letter to the queen. Might not he be in the wrong, after all ? Was there no means of saving his life without imperilling his soul ? Had he not a right of appeal from the Pope to a general council of the Church ? But again, if obedience to the Pope were wrong in itself, might it not become a duty when it was enjoined by the sovereign ? His old belief in royal infallibility had to be remembered. Royal command set forth what religion he was to accept. He had obeyed the royal command, whether or no it ran counter to his private convictions, in the reign of Henry. Was he to disobey in the reign of Henry's daughter ?

Pole noted, exulted in, and used every sign of wavering. Neither he nor Mary had the slightest intention of sparing Cranmer's life. But his conversion was almost as desirable as his death. If he could be induced to leave a full recantation behind him, its influence upon other heretics would be immense. Therefore Pole spared no effort to obtain it. In such a business he could command the expert assistance of the Spanish friars. Cranmer was treated with a show of kindness. He was removed from gaol and lodged in the deanery of Christ Church. While nothing that could be claimed as a promise was made, he was given to understand that by putting his name to an adequate submission he could save his life. Spanish friars were sent to threaten or beguile him. Towards the end of January 1556 he signed his first submission, which ran :

Forasmuch as the king's and queen's majesties, by consent of their parliament, have received the Pope's authority within this realm, I am content to submit myself to their laws herein, and to take the Pope for chief head of the Church of England, so far as God's laws and the laws and customs of this realm will permit.

Soon followed another, in less guarded terms :

I, Thomas Cranmer, doctor in divinity, do submit myself to the Catholic Church of Christ, and to the Pope, supreme Head of the same Church, and unto the king's and the queen's majesties, and unto all their laws and ordinances.

But the formal sentence of condemnation

from Rome had arrived, and on February 14 Bonner, Bishop of London, and Thirlby, Bishop of Ely, came to degrade him formally from Holy Orders. The brutal ceremonial was performed with tears of compassion by his friend Thirlby, with indecent truculence by Bonner. Cranmer vainly endeavoured to thrust upon them his appeal to a general council. From the welcome alleviations of the deanery he was sent back to the common gaol. There he signed two further " submissions ", not differing greatly from those to which he had already set his name. On February 24 the writ for his execution arrived. He was to die on March 7.

But Pole and the friars did not wish him to escape their grasp until he had made a complete recantation. So far he had professed submission to the Pope, but had not explicitly accepted papal doctrines or condemned his own. So far, too, he had written in English, and Latin was needed for a document to be circulated far and wide among the Continental heretics. Then, under the shadow of death, Cranmer's last remnant of fortitude gave way. He wrote, or at least copied and signed with his own hand, an abject surrender of every principle he held and of every truth he believed. He promised that, if only a short reprieve could be allowed him, he would sign one yet more abject. Pole was ready enough to grant him another fortnight of life on such terms, and probably himself drafted the final recantation. When Cranmer had signed it he had accepted not only the papal claims in their entirety, but the doctrines of transubstantiation and purgatory. He had denounced himself as sole author of Henry's divorce and the innumerable ills springing from it. He said that he had opened the window to all heresies, of which he himself was the chief teacher. He had robbed the dead of their masses. He had more than deserved all the pains of hell. But nothing less than a full translation of this revolting document could convey a just idea of its nauseous imagery, of the depths of self-degradation to which it descended.

It was signed in vain. The miserable fortnight it had purchased drew to a close. There was to be no further reprieve. On the eve of March 21 the stake was made ready. The pitiful account of its cost is still extant : " For an hundred of wood - faggots, six shillings ; for an hundred - and - a - half of furze-faggots, three shillings and fourpence ; for the carriage of them, eightpence ; to two labourers, one and fourpence "—eleven shillings and fourpence in all. Dr. Coles, Provost of Eton, who had been ordered by the queen to preach the execution sermon on the morrow, visited the prisoner. He still adhered to his final recantation. After Coles' departure Cranmer spent his time upon a manuscript from which he would read next day. He sent requests to some of the colleges for funeral masses. A message of farewell came from one of his sisters ; a message the more poignant because she was yet loyal to the views which Cranmer had abjured.

March 21 dawned. It was a day of pelting rain. Therefore the authorities ordered that the sermon should be preached in St. Mary's, and not, after the usual custom, beside the stake. A platform on which the prisoner would stand was hastily put up opposite the pulpit. He received absolution in the prison. Thence, about nine o'clock, he was led to his place in the church, walking between two friars. As he entered, the strains of the *Nunc dimittis* extinguished his last hope of reprieve. Cole performed his odious task not unkindly, and bade Cranmer hope for an entrance into Paradise like that vouchsafed to the penitent thief. Then he bade the crowd hear and pray with the prisoner.

Cranmer drew forth his manuscript from the ragged gown in which he was clothed. First, he knelt and read a prayer. Then, with his eyes still on his paper, he stood and addressed the people. " Every man desireth at the time of their deaths," he began, " to give some good exhortation, that other may remember and be the better thereby. So I beseech God grant me grace that I may speak something at this my departing whereby God may be glorified and you edified." He bade them love God, obey the king and queen willingly and gladly, and live in unity. Next he charged the wealthy to be charitable, " for if ever they had any occasion to show their charity, they have now at this present, the poor people being so many and victuals so dear ". Then he said he would declare his " very faith, how I believe, without colour or dissimulation. For now is no time to dissemble, whatsoever I have written in times past." First, he avowed his unaltered acceptance of the Catholic faith, and of every word taught by Christ, His Apostles, and Prophets.

Thus he reached the passage in his manuscript which ran :

" And now I come to the great thing that troubleth my conscience more than any other thing I ever did, and that is the setting abroad of

writings contrary to the truth, which here now
I renounce "—

and went on to state that these erroneous
writings were " the books which I wrote
against the sacrament of the altar since the
death of King Henry VIII ". But at the
word " renounce " he paused. He raised
his eyes from the written paper. He looked
at the people. Slowly and deliberately he
went on :

—renounce and refuse as things written with my
hand contrary to the truth I thought in my heart,
and writ for fear of death, and to save my life, if it
might be—and that is all such bills as I have written
or signed with mine own hand since my degradation,
wherein I have written many things untrue. And
forasmuch as my hand offended in writing contrary
to my heart, therefore my hand shall first be
punished ; for if I may come to the fire, it shall be
first burned. And as for the Pope, I refuse him, as
Christ's enemy and antichrist, with all his false
doctrines.

He would have said more. But the
amazed silence was now broken by a storm
of words—cries of wonder and fierce protest, and, it may well be, of sympathy also.
Dr. Coles ordered him to cease. He was
dragged down from his platform and out of
the church. But he eluded the gaolers'
grasp, and hurried so fast towards the stake
that the panting and expostulating friars

could not keep pace with him. Soon they ceased their pleadings, saying that he was possessed of the devil. He was fastened to the stake and the faggots were kindled. He thrust his right hand into the rising flame, crying " This hand hath offended ! " They were his last words. Thereafter he neither spoke nor moved, and, with merciful swiftness, the end came.

Such was the life of Thomas Cranmer. More was wrought for its popular fame by its last minutes than by all its previous years. To multitudes Cranmer is familiar only as the archbishop who was burnt, and at the stake thrust his hand into the fire. As we close the tragic record, we need not linger to estimate his character afresh. Yet we may remember that the office he held and the age in which he lived were of a kind to accentuate his faults and to obscure his merits. It is his public career which emphasises his lamentable failings. It is his private correspondence which demonstrates his eager and ready kindliness. Among all his numerous letters to Cromwell, for instance, there is scarcely one that does not ask a favour, not for himself but for some friend or humble dependant. In judging his public work, again, we must not underestimate the difficulties of his position. Unquestionably he was a weak archbishop. Yet a strong archbishop would probably have lost his place under Edward if he had not already forfeited his life under Henry. The deposition of Cranmer in Edward's reign might have meant the installation of a revolutionary like Hooper or of a fanatic like Knox. Such a change would soon have converted the ancient Church into a novel sect. In a sense, this danger was averted by Cranmer's weakness. His few acts of courage were the more effective because they were wholly unexpected. The opportunity for them was given him because Henry and Northumberland believed that they could rely safely on his cowardice.

None the less, when all such pleas have been urged and every allowance made, an impartial judgment cannot affirm that Cranmer was either a great man or a great archbishop. It will prefer to say that he was thrust into an office for which he had as little desire as fitness, and that the trials of office reacted disastrously upon his strangely plastic character. It will not seek to exculpate him from censure which is but too well deserved. It will insist that evil wrought is not less evil when it is done under mistaken theories or with excellent intentions. Yet this impartial judgement will not forget the skill and patient toil which enriched our national life with the Book of Common Prayer. And in taking leave of Thomas Cranmer, it will think of him kindly, not as a model primate, not as an example of virtue, but as a very fallible and ill-starred man, of whose story it may be said with truth that the annals of our Church hold few more interesting, and none more pathetic.

INDEX

THE END

Printed in Great Britain by R. & R. CLARK, LIMITED, *Edinburgh.*